Cannelle et Vanille

Nourishing, Gluten-Free Recipes
for Every Meal and Mood

Written and photographed by
Aran Goyoaga

SASQUATCH BOOKS

SEATTLE

For Jon and Miren

———————

I hope you will always think of me in
the kitchen with an apron on.

Contents

A Cook's Remedy: An Introduction 1
Stocking the Pantry and Tools to Use 5

CHAPTER ONE
Pantry Staples 17

Nut Milk 20
Coconut Milk 21
Hemp Milk 21
Cultured Butter 24
Crème Fraîche 26
Simple Nut or Seed Butter 28
Chocolate-Hazelnut Butter 29
Whole-Milk Yogurt 32
Mayonnaise 34
Labneh 37
Dukkah 40
Mix-and-Match Granola 43
Pickled Vegetables 44
Shrubs and Drinking Vinegars 47
Preserved Lemons 48
Chicken Stock 53
Beef Stock 54
Fish Stock 55
Vegetable Stock 56
Gluten-Free Sourdough Starter 59

CHAPTER TWO
Morning 63

Ginger-Turmeric Milk 66
Spicy Carrot-Grapefruit Juice 68
Turmeric Detox Broth with Swiss Chard 71
Roasted Cherries with Coconut Granola 72
Bircher Muesli with Poached Rhubarb and Hazelnuts 74
Grilled Peaches with Cashew Cream on Toast 77
Cinnamon Buns 78
Avocado, Smoked Salmon, and Cucumber on Toast 81
Rice Pudding with Plums 82

Soft-Cooked Eggs with Dukkah and Bitter Greens
    on Toast 85
Baked Eggs in Piperrada 86
Egg Tostada with Fennel, Radishes, and Yogurt 88
Sourdough Waffles with Carmelized Peaches 91
Buckwheat Crêpes with Chocolate-Hazelnut Butter 92
Raspberry Pancakes with Maple Yogurt 95

CHAPTER THREE
Baking 97

Nordic Rye-Style Seed Bread 101
Sourdough Boules 103
Buckwheat Sweet Yeast Bread with Dried Apricots
    and Walnuts 109
Black Olive, Caraway, and Honey Yeast Bread 110
Plum Frangipane Tart 112
Caramelized Apple Galette 117
Fig, Taleggio, and Pine Nut Tart 123
Gâteau Basque 124
One-Bowl Apricot and Olive Oil Cake 128
Apple Cider Yeast Doughnuts 130
Roasted Squash Brown Butter Cake 135
Banana Bread with Sunflower Seed Icing 136
Flaky Caramelized Onion and Fennel Biscuits 139
Parsnip and Ginger Cake with Cultured Butter
    and Crème Fraîche Icing 142

CHAPTER FOUR
Midday 145

Winter Salad with Roasted Radicchio, Avocados,
    and Hazelnut Dukkah 148
Spicy Chicken Salad with Apple, Celery, and
    Pickled Vegetables 151
Buttermilk-Poached Salmon Salad with Herb, Leek,
    and Caper Dressing 152
Shaved Beet and Lentil Salad with Tahini and
    Preserved Lemon Dressing 155
Simple Asparagus and Avocado Soup 157
Roasted Carrot and Cashew Soup 158
Peas and Ham with Buttermilk Dressing 160
Melon, Serrano, Fennel, and Ricotta Salata 163
Tomato, Corn, and Bread Salad 164
Mushrooms and Eggs 167
Crunchy Romaine Salad with Soft Eggs and Feta 168
Black Rice Bowl with Figs, Radicchio, Pickled Radishes,
    and Pepitas 171

CHAPTER FIVE
Everyday Dinners 173

Roasted Carrots with Red Lentil Hummus 176
Tomato and Romesco Tart 180
My Niçoise Salad 183
Tortilla de Patatas with Romaine, Fennel, and Green
    Olive Salad 184
Crispy Chickpeas with Rice, Sweet Potatoes, Avocados,
    and Greens 188
Squash, Leek, and Potato Soup with Cheese Toast 191
Roasted Cauliflower, Swiss Chard, and Hazelnut Pasta 192
Lentil and Root Vegetable Stew with Broccoli Rabe
    and Fried Eggs 195
Spaghetti and Meatballs 198
Crispy Snapper with Root Veggie Mash 199
Spicy Lamb Sausage with Yogurt, Herbs,
    and Fried Egg 203
Braised Chicken with Apples and Cider 205
Slow-Roasted Salmon with Fennel, Citrus,
    and Harissa 206

CHAPTER SIX
The Gathering Table 209

A SPANISH GATHERING 213
Chicken and Seafood Paella on an Open Fire 214
Grilled Green Tomato and Eggplant Salad 218
Peach Txakoli Cocktail 219

HOMEMADE PASTA DINNER 227
Homemade Pasta 228
Braised Beef Ragù with Tagliatelle 232
Radicchio, Apple, and Celery Root Salad with
    Buttermilk–Poppy Seed Vinaigrette 233

THE GARDEN AND THE SEA 237
My Mom's Fish Soup 238
Aioli and Gruyère Tartines 240
Peppery Greens with Mustard-Honey Vinaigrette 240

VEGETARIAN HARVEST GATHERING 245
Ricotta Gnudi with Slow-Roasted Tomatoes 247
Roasted Squash Salad with White Beans, Bread Crumbs,
    and Preserved Lemon 248
Ginger-Fennel Tonic 249

GRILLED BACKYARD PIZZAS 253
Pizza Dough 254
Squash Blossom and Ricotta Pizza 257
Tomato, Prosciutto, and Red Onion Pizza 258
Leek, Fennel, and Pesto Pizza 259
Blistered Corn, Nectarine, and Watercress Salad 263
Mashed Berries in Lillet 265

SUNDAY ROASTED CHICKEN 267
Buttermilk-Brined Roasted Chicken 268
Roasted Potatoes the English Way with Tarragon Aioli 269
Artichoke, Fennel, Sugar Snap Pea, and Parmesan Salad 273

CELEBRATING WITH OYSTERS AND STEAK 275
Oysters with Champagne Mignonette 277
The Perfect Steak with Garlic and Red Chili Flakes 279
Shaved Asparagus, Cucumber, and Pistachio Salad 283

CHAPTER SEVEN
Desserts and Small Indulgences 285

Quince Paste 292
Amama Miren's Flan 297
Apricots in Honey and Saffron 299
Chocolate, Olive Oil, and Citrus Cake 301
Roasted Pears with Seed Crumble 303
Buttermilk Panna Cotta with Summer Fruits 307
Chocolate Cream with Yogurt, Cocoa Nibs, and
    Raspberries 308
Peach and Hibiscus Sorbet 311
Espresso and No-Churn Honey Ice Cream 312
Frozen Raspberry Custard with Hazelnut Crunch 314
Orange and Brown Butter Madeleines 318
Salted Hazelnut Butter Truffles 321
Salted Apple Cider Caramels 322

Acknowledgments 325
Online Resources 327
Index 331

A Cook's Remedy: An Introduction

My earliest memory is the scent of *cannelle et vanille*: cinnamon and vanilla. My small three-year-old hands clutched my grandmother Miren's waist as I tottered, tiptoed, on the green stool she had pulled up beside her. She was my mother's mother, a pastry chef who was rarely far from the kitchen. She would spend hours there, with me at her side, pasteurizing the raw milk she bought from the dairy up the street. The pot would simmer on the stovetop, and the cream that would rise to the top was scooped out and spread heavily atop toast, finished with a sprinkle of cinnamon. But one of my favorite dishes was the steaming pots of *arroz con leche*, a creamy rice pudding, that same familiar scent of vanilla and cinnamon wrapping me up like the warmest blanket.

I grew up in a small Basque town called Amorebieta in northern Spain. My roots in the region are deep. In 1949, my grandparents, Angel and Miren, opened the only artisanal pastry shop in the village, Pastelería Ayarza. Some thirty years later, I would spend my youth in that very kitchen, spreading sugary, rich buttercream on rows and rows of delicate cookies.

Cooking defined my family. Between the pastry shop and the hours spent in our home kitchen, food provided a through line that extended between generations. It was as much a part of our family's shared identity as our Basque heritage. In my teenage years, as I searched for my own identity, I denied the pull of the kitchen and developed a secret eating disorder that haunted me for years. I felt compelled to separate from my family, to establish myself as an independent entity, so I left the Basque Country. I left the kitchen. I left everything my family held dear.

I covered a lot of ground in that journey. I landed in the United States, married my American husband, and lived in several cities across the country. I worked a few unfulfilling corporate jobs to put my business degree to use, but something was missing. Meanwhile, as I was striving to recover from my eating disorder, I found surprisingly that the kitchen became a refuge—a familiar place where I could be creative, nourish my body, and feel comforted. Ultimately, I could not escape its allure: it was my remedy. I stepped out of my self-imposed isolation and into my self-expression. I realized that cooking was in my blood all along and that I, too, wanted to be defined by it.

It was when my husband and I moved from Colorado to Florida that I finally found the courage to leave my career in business and enroll in a culinary school's pastry program. I worked as a pastry cook at night in several restaurants until I ended up in the pastry kitchen of a five-star hotel for three years. Then, in 2006, my son was born and things changed. The long hours and physical nature of the work didn't allow me enough time to care for my family, so I quit the professional kitchen. While I was raising my son and contemplating my next move, I started a blog, *Cannelle et Vanille*, which took me in a new, unexpected direction of writing and photography. After my daughter was born a couple of years later, I was diagnosed with Hashimoto's and Ménière's disease, and also discovered I had a gluten intolerance.

Today I live in Seattle with my husband and two children. My blog paved the way for a career as a photographer and food stylist, so most of my time now is spent in the kitchen—though my bright, open studio is very different from the warm, cramped space of my youth. The combination of Seattle dreariness and a photographer's yearning for light drew me to the space in a hundred-year-old former stable with creaky steps and an ancient industrial elevator, just up the street from the historic Pike Place Market and down the hill from my home. I've spent years honing it into the perfect intersection of practicality and inspiration.

In my life, cooking is a form of therapy, a space for self-expression, introspection, and self-discovery. It's a remedy to silence my ever-anxious mind through the simplicity of a repetitive task. Beyond its preparation, the cooking experience wouldn't be complete without friends and family to revel in my food, encouraging conversation around the table and, ultimately, creating a safe space for vulnerability and truth.

The recipes I enjoy at home with my loved ones are exactly the ones I share with you in this book. My cooking philosophy is one of balance. I eat whole foods—a wide variety of vegetables and fruits, as well as plant and animal proteins—and I give a bit of space and permission for small indulgences. As such, the dishes included here reflect many different sides of my cooking personality. My goal has been to create recipes that are approachable and not overly aspirational. They are also meant to inspire you and act as a foundational element in your kitchen. You will be able to take bits and pieces from each page and use them to create your own twist. Shift the candied nuts from a salad recipe into a roasted vegetable bowl. Try a variety of fruits in a frangipane tart. Experiment with different ingredients in a paella once you understand the technique and how to build the proper fire.

This cookbook is oriented around a day in my kitchen, because over the course of a single day, food takes on many different meanings. Food is a nourishing ritual, especially in the early morning hours, and is more functional on weeknight evenings when time seems to move more quickly. On a relaxed weekend, I fall into the methodical lull of kneading breads and crafting pastries, and embrace the intricacies of more time-consuming gatherings and meal-ending desserts. I encourage you to knead, roll, and cut fresh pasta (page 228) on a quiet weekend morning in preparation for what will become a bustling evening with friends. Or late at night, when everyone has already gone to bed, feed your sourdough starter (page 59) and measure all the ingredients for the next day's comforting breakfast of Sourdough Waffles with Carmelized Peaches (page 91).

As much as I cherish my alone time in the kitchen, I realize friends and family love to help and participate in the creative process, so I put them to work as well. Children measure and whisk all the ingredients for the tarragon aioli to serve alongside the Buttermilk-Brined Roasted Chicken (page 268) and Roasted Potatoes the English Way (page 269). I leave those who take pride in building fires in charge of getting the Green Egg going for pizzas (page 253). And I am never shy about asking guests to help clean up as the evening comes to a close.

My hope, dear reader, is to share my love for cooking, which has been a remedy for many physical and emotional growing pains in my life. I hope this book will likewise inspire you on your own path of nourishment as well as in connections to yourself and to others. Revel in the simple dishes and embrace the challenge of the more elaborate ones. Preparing meals alone or together is a meaningful, rewarding, and—dare I say—transformational act.

Stocking the Pantry and Tools to Use

PANTRY INGREDIENTS

The kitchen shelves in my studio are lined with clear mason jars filled with different types of flours, spices, sweeteners, and other pantry staples. It helps me keep the pantry organized and clean. Most of the ingredients listed below are available at most supermarkets and health-food shops, and whatever I cannot find in a brick-and-mortar store, I order online.

Flours

BUCKWHEAT FLOUR. Despite its name, buckwheat is not a true grain but a fruit seed. It has a nutty, distinct flavor. You can buy buckwheat flour already milled, but since buckwheat groats are quite soft, I like to process the flour at home using a high-speed blender. You can find raw groats or roasted ones, also called kasha—I prefer raw for flour.

NUT FLOUR. Nut flour adds fat and loads of flavor to baked goods such as cakes, quick breads, and cookies. My two favorite nut flours for baking are almond flour and hazelnut flour. I make my nut flours in a high-speed blender by grinding the nuts in small amounts because the heat of the blender can alter their texture and make them slightly oily. When I make nut milks (see page 20), I save the pulp that is left behind after straining the liquid, dry it, grind it once more, and then use it as a flour as well.

OAT FLOUR. Oats, which are naturally gluten-free, are often processed along with wheat, which can cause some people to react to the cross contamination. Look for certified gluten-free oat flour, or make your own at home using rolled oats. I use oat flour in my sourdough boule and pancake recipes, which adds great texture, so don't worry if your flour is not finely milled.

Why My Recipes Are Gluten-Free and How to Substitute

If you are new to my work, you might be surprised to find that all the recipes in this book are gluten-free. After each of my pregnancies, I developed autoimmune disorders (Hashimoto's and Ménière's, respectively), which left me debilitated for several months. In 2010, I discovered I have a genetic gluten intolerance; I have been cooking and eating exclusively without gluten ever since.

If gluten isn't a problem for you, my recipes can be made using wheat flour, because most baking recipes, except yeast breads (see page 105 for a note in this regard), are easy to convert. Simply add up the total weight of all the gluten-free flour measurements and substitute that same amount of all-purpose wheat flour. It's that simple. Note that there are two recipes that use xanthan gum: Flaky Caramelized Onion and Fennel Biscuits (page 139) and Puff Pastry (page 119). If you are converting those recipes for all-purpose flour, simply omit the xanthan gum as it's there to give the gluten-free recipe structure and therefore not necessary for gluten flours.

POTATO STARCH. Not to be confused with potato flour, potato starch is a starch that I like to mix with other whole-grain flours to help produce a soft texture in baked goods.

SORGHUM FLOUR. This slightly sweet, high-protein flour works well in bread recipes. Sorghum flour is yellowish in color and soft in texture, so it blends well with other whole-grain and nut flours.

SUPERFINE BROWN RICE FLOUR. This is probably the most vital ingredient in my baking recipes. I rely on it heavily because of its finely milled texture, which allows liquids to be absorbed well, resulting in baked goods less prone to being crunchy and overly crumbly. The downside is that a superfine grind is not as readily available as other rice flours. My go-to brand is Authentic Foods (see page 328), which is not as readily available as other brands (check their website for retailers). Regular brown rice flour can be substituted in my recipes, but the end product will be a bit crumblier and its texture slightly coarser.

SUPERFINE SWEET RICE FLOUR. Also known as glutinous flour, this flour is ground from very starchy, "sticky" short-grain white rice. It is very thickening, which makes a great binding agent. It has a mild, slightly sweet flavor. As with brown rice flour, I prefer a superfine grind, but a regular grind will work in its place.

TAPIOCA STARCH. Tapioca starch is also commonly referred to as tapioca flour. It is a thickener I often recommend for individuals who cannot tolerate corn. I use it in combination with other whole-grain flours to add lightness. It binds well and creates a nice crust in baked goods.

Binders

FLAXSEED MEAL. I use flaxseed as a binder in bread recipes because, when mixed with liquid, it gels and acts like glue. I grind my own flaxseed meal at home, processing small amounts at a time since the seeds, like nuts, have quite a bit of oil, and the texture changes when overheated. Flaxseed can also be used as an egg substitute when baking. Mix 1 tablespoon ground flax-seed with 2 tablespoons hot water in place of each egg called for. This works particularly well in cakes and quick breads.

PSYLLIUM HUSK POWDER. Psyllium husks come from the seed of the plantago plant, a native of India and Pakistan. They are a great source of soluble fiber and can absorb high amounts of moisture, which make the powder a perfect ingredient to help add elasticity to gluten-free yeasted breads in need of strength and structure. Psyllium is usually available in large supermarkets with an extensive health-food section and specialty stores, but you can also order it online.

XANTHAN GUM. I am a bit conflicted about xanthan gum because the process used to make it is a bit more chemical than I am comfortable with. It seems to be hard for some peo-ple to digest as well. However, there are certain recipes in this book that need a little of it for more structure and a successful outcome, such as the Flaky Caramelized Onion and Fennel Biscuits (page 139), Homemade Pasta (page 228), and Puff Pastry (page 119). I try to use it as minimally as possible.

Fats

BUTTER. Due to a sensitivity to dairy, I reserve butter only for pastry that really needs it. In general, I like to buy butter made from grass-fed cream that has a higher fat content than normal. It makes it pliable and extremely yellow. You can also find a recipe for cultured butter on page 24. It's delicious spread over bread as well.

COCONUT OIL AND BUTTER. Coconut oil is the oil that is extracted from coconut meat, and coconut butter is coconut meat that has been pulverized to a spreadable consistency. I use coconut oil for baking and coconut butter for spreading on bread or blending into drinks.

DAIRY-FREE BUTTER. My son cannot have any dairy at all because it triggers migraines for him. When I bake for him, I use Earth Balance's soy-free butter. It is interchangeable with regular butter.

OLIVE OIL. I grew up with nothing but olive oil. I cannot recall a time when my mom used any other vegetable oil or cooked with butter. She lightly fried with olive oil, she used it on salads, and she baked with it. It is in my genes. I take great pleasure in olive oil that comes from small makers and treat is as a delicacy. There are always several bottles of olive oil in my pantry—ones I have purchased and ones that have been gifted to me. Not all oils are equal, so make sure you taste them. Some olives have fruity profiles and others are very strong and peppery. I see it as a matter of personal preference as to how you use them. I personally stay away from bottles labeled "light," because they have been refined and have lost so many of the qualities I love about olive oil.

Sweeteners

HONEY. I always shop for unfiltered raw honey at my local farmers' market. It is antibacterial, antifungal, and full of antioxidants. Every morning I mix water, fresh lemon juice, and raw honey as a booster before I do anything else, and I love it in vinaigrettes and baked goods.

LIGHT BROWN SUGAR. This is simply refined white sugar with molasses added back into it, creating a darker, coarser, moister sugar. I like to use it primarily in cakes, quick breads, and cookies.

MOLASSES. Molasses is a thick, dark-brown syrup obtained from raw sugar during the refining process. It adds moisture, color, and a slight bitterness to cakes, cookies, and breads.

NATURAL CANE SUGAR. The recipes in this book that call for sugar have all been made with natural cane sugar. It is slightly coarser than refined white sugar but works the same.

Salt

FLAKY SEA SALT. I use sea salt mostly for finishing, but in some baking recipes, I'll add it for crunch and a different minerality. Maldon is what I usually have on my counter, along with Brittany's *fleur de sel* and *flor de sal* from Salinas de Añana in the Basque Country.

KOSHER SALT. I have different kinds of salts from all the places I visit, but kosher salt is my everyday salt. I have listed specific measurements for all my recipes; however, note that all salts taste different, so use your discretion to adjust salt amounts, except when baking (which will affect the outcome).

Eggs

The eggs listed in this book are large, which weigh approximately 1.5 ounces (45 grams) each. I get my eggs at the farmers' market, where I shop for deep-orange yolks, which indicate the hens' rich, nutrient-heavy diet. I am also lucky that I have a few friends with chickens, and in the summer months when they lay abundantly, I am gifted dozens of different colors. I recognize that this is quite a luxury and not everyone has access to eggs from free-roaming chickens, so supermarket options will do, of course.

Spices

I buy spices in small amounts from a local spice shop that sells them in bulk, and also from the bulk section at the supermarket. In general, I prefer to buy seeds whole and grind them myself in a dedicated coffee grinder just prior to using them—this ensures potency and freshness.

PIMENT D'ESPELETTE. This sweet, smoky, and slightly spicy ground pepper is called for in many of the recipes here because it is a quintessential Basque spice. It originates from the village of Espelette in the French side of the Basque Country. The red peppers are harvested and hung to dry in windows all over the town. You can find the ground pepper in specialty shops that sell French and Spanish delicacies. Aleppo pepper, another of my favorites, is a good substitute for it, or in a pinch, an equal mix of smoked paprika and cayenne.

VANILLA BEANS. I buy vanilla beans in bulk from my local spice shop, and again, I only buy what I need because they tend to dry out over time. Be sure to seek out vanilla beans that are plump and moist. The flesh should be sticky and full of a million tiny little seeds. There are many varieties depending on the country of origin, so explore your options. If extra beans are unavoidable, I triple-wrap the extras in plastic or air-seal them to keep them fresh longer. If you don't have access to vanilla beans, you can use 3 teaspoons of vanilla extract or 1½ teaspoons of vanilla powder in place of one whole bean.

KITCHEN TOOLS

I am a minimalist when it comes to kitchen tools. I shy away from single-use items like a garlic press or strawberry huller. I find they only create clutter and don't really reduce prep time much. Instead, I focus on having great knives, which doesn't mean expensive knives; a high-speed blender and a stand mixer, each with a strong motor; quality tart and cake pans; and two heavy-duty Dutch ovens (a 9-quart and a 5-quart). Think of your tools as investments, and acquire quality pieces that will last you most of a lifetime.

CAST-IRON DUTCH OVEN. I do most of my cooking in enameled cast-iron Dutch ovens. I have a large 9-quart pot for making soups and stews or braising bigger cuts of meat. Cast-iron is especially perfect for gas stoves. If you have an electric stove, it's still great, but you will be able to really tell the difference when you have flames. Cast-iron holds heat for a long time. I also have two smaller 5-quart cast-iron Dutch ovens that I use to bake my sourdough bread in. Because they are uncoated, I season them with flaxseed oil every other time so they don't rust. There are many great brands out there, such as Le Creuset, Staub, Lodge—I am a fan of them all.

HIGH-SPEED BLENDER. A quality high-speed blender will change your life. For a long time, I hesitated to make the investment as they aren't cheap, but I am glad I did. I have used mine multiple times a day, every single day, for the past ten years. Mine is a Vitamix, and it's the only brand I have ever owned. I use it to blend soups and smoothies, mill flours, make nut butters and milks, and puree all kinds of pastes.

KITCHEN SCALE. If you own nothing else on this tool list, at least purchase a kitchen scale. If you bake and want to be successful every single time, it is essential to have one, and the cost is minimal. I know many home cooks are not used to weighing ingredients, but I highly encourage everyone that loves to bake to stop using volume measurements altogether. While testing these recipes, I noticed that two different sets of measuring cups gave me two different weights of flour. In some recipes, the variance is not that important, but when you are dealing with doughs, a bit more or less flour can have a big impact. Weighing ingredients results in consistent outcomes—trust me on this one.

KNIVES. A chef's knife, a paring knife, and a serrated knife are the only three knives I need. You may also want a fillet knife if you do a lot of fish filleting, or a boning knife for butchering. The price range for knives is vast and so is the quality. I often find that restaurant supply shops carry exactly the right middle range of options. Knives that are not crazy expensive but are solidly built from quality materials (and regularly sharpened) will last for a long time.

OVEN THERMOMETER. The stove I used to create and test these recipes had a gas range and an electric oven. Because all cooktops and ovens are slightly different, I recommend using an oven thermometer, especially for baking. Cooking times could also vary.

PASTRY TOOLS. A bench scraper is always by my side when I am making bread or doughs. A proofing basket or *banneton* can be used to shape breads, though you can always use a bowl instead. I also find a pastry brush handy for an egg wash or oil, as well as to brush excess flour from doughs.

STAINLESS STEEL SAUTÉ PANS. All-Clad is my go-to brand for stainless steel pans—my preferred choice for stovetop cooking. Although I don't own any, I have also cooked with and enjoyed carbon-steel pans, but note that these need to be seasoned just like cast iron.

STAND MIXER. I am a pastry chef at heart, so I couldn't live without a stand mixer. I use mine with all the attachments for mixing dough, creaming cookies, or whipping meringue. Yes, you could do a lot of these by hand, but it's so much faster with the stand mixer. Mine is a refurbished KitchenAid that I got when I was in culinary school fifteen years ago. It's a 6-quart version, so very roomy. It's been my companion for all these years, and its motor has survived daily use.

TART AND CAKE PANS. Because I am a pastry chef, I have acquired a multitude of pans throughout the years, but honestly my favorites are a 9-inch cake pan from Nordic Ware, another 9-inch tart pan with removable bottom from Matfer, and a rectangle loaf pan from USA Pan. My preference is for uncoated stainless steel.

VOLUME MEASURING CUPS. All the liquid measures in this book are displayed using volume cups. However, because there can be inconsistencies when using volume, I recommend weighing them instead (see page 105).

CHAPTER ONE

Pantry
Staples

My recipes adapt to the seasons and integrate nature's offerings, but there are always staples in my pantry and refrigerator that serve as the building blocks for my cooking. I'll buy canned coconut milk at the supermarket or tahini from the corner store, and I definitely don't always churn my own cultured butter. But there is something very grounding about starting from scratch at home. Creating these foundational elements in my own kitchen allows me to get to know my taste and technique more deeply, and it is freeing to be so self-reliant. Take the opportunity to explore your own likes and dislikes: Do you prefer thicker yogurt, saltier nut butter, sweeter granola? Once you have constructed these basics, you can apply that same approach to refining and reshaping so many other dishes, developing a connection to your food.

In this chapter you will find foundational recipes that are referenced throughout the book. Nut milks make an appearance in multiple baked goods and desserts; cultured butter can be spread on toasted bread or used to create pastry doughs with a slight tang; sourdough starter makes for delicious waffles, Nordic-style bread, or the boule I bake thrice weekly for my family; tahini is stirred into red lentil hummus and salad dressings; shrubs act as a base for cocktails; and, one of my favorites, pickled vegetables adorn all kinds of salads.

Nut Milk

1 cup (about 150 g) raw nuts
(almonds, cashews, hazelnuts,
pistachios, pecans, walnuts,
peanuts)
3 cups (675 g) filtered water
1 tablespoon maple syrup or
honey, or 2 dates (optional)
½ teaspoon vanilla extract
(optional)
⅛ teaspoon kosher salt

Note: The resulting nut pulp can
be turned into nut flour. Spread
the pulp over a baking sheet
lined with parchment paper and
place in the oven with the oven
light on overnight, or longer if
needed, until completely dry.
Alternatively, you can use a
dehydrator. Once dry, grind the
nut pulp in a high-speed blender
or food processor to a fine
powder. I use the flour in cakes
and cookies.

I have been making nut milks ever since discovering my son's
intolerance to casein, which is the protein in cow's milk (as well
as goat's and sheep's). There are countless options available in
supermarkets now, but most of them have binders and emulsi-
fiers to extend shelf life, and they tend to be more expensive
than making them at home. You can use just about any nut, but in
general I tend to use almonds, cashews, and hazelnuts the most.

Even though the instructions that follow indicate to do so, I
don't always strain my cashew milk as the nuts are very soft and
hardly leave any sediment behind. However, if you plan to use
cashew milk to cook with (for example, in a rice pudding), make
sure you do strain it or the nut pulp can burn at the bottom of
the pan.

MAKES 1 QUART

1 In a large bowl, combine the nuts with enough cold tap water
to cover them by 2 inches. Soak the nuts for 8 to 12 hours at
room temperature (I usually do this overnight).

2 Drain the nuts and discard the soaking water. Transfer the
nuts to a high-speed blender, and add the filtered water, sweetener of choice, vanilla, and salt. Blend on high until smooth and
creamy, about 2 minutes.

3 Line a strainer with cheesecloth and position over a medium
bowl (or use a nut milk bag). Strain the liquid, then bring the
cheesecloth edges together and give it a good, tight squeeze
with clean hands to release all the milk.

4 Transfer the milk to a glass bottle with a lid and store in the
refrigerator for up to 4 days.

Coconut Milk

The process for coconut milk is similar to that of nut milk, but there is no need to soak the coconut overnight. I keep my coconut milk very simple and don't sweeten or flavor it. It is my go-to for coffee because it's rich and creamy.

MAKES 1 QUART

3 cups (235 g) unsweetened shredded coconut
4 cups (900 g) hot (not boiling) filtered water

1 Combine the coconut and filtered water in a high-speed blender, and let it soak for 10 minutes. Blend on high speed until creamy, about 2 minutes.

2 Line a strainer with cheesecloth and position over a medium bowl (or use a nut milk bag). Strain the liquid, then bring the cheesecloth edges together and give it a good, tight squeeze with clean hands to release all the milk.

3 Transfer the milk to a glass bottle with a lid and store in the refrigerator for up to 4 days. Coconut milk tends to separate as it sits; if that happens, give it a good shake before using.

Hemp Milk

Hemp seeds are incredibly beneficial for the skin and the heart with high omega-3 content. Hemp milk also doesn't require overnight soaking, making it a quick milk option. It is not as rich as other nut milks, and its grassy taste might not be everyone's cup of tea.

MAKES 1 QUART

3 cups (675 g) filtered water
1 cup (150 g) raw shelled hemp seeds
1 tablespoon maple syrup or honey, or 2 dates (optional)
½ teaspoon vanilla extract (optional)
⅛ teaspoon kosher salt

1 Combine all the ingredients in a high-speed blender and blend until creamy, 1 to 2 minutes. You can strain hemp milk, but I don't find it necessary.

2 Transfer the milk to a glass bottle with a lid and store in the refrigerator for up to 4 days.

Cultured Butter

2 cups (450 g) heavy cream
2 tablespoons (30 g) cultured buttermilk or cultured whole-milk yogurt
¼ to ½ teaspoon flaky sea salt (optional)

I love the tangy flavor and golden, velvety texture of cultured butter. It's worth the extra time to make your own, especially for use in a pastry such as puff or pie dough. Or, even more simply, let it be the star with a hearty slather over toasted sourdough bread.

Use 1 tablespoon cultured buttermilk or yogurt per 1 cup heavy cream. Don't skimp on the heavy cream—use the best product you can find with the highest fat content, ideally from grass-fed cows. Avoid any cream that contains thickeners.

MAKES APPROXIMATELY 7 OUNCES (200 G)

1 Whisk together the heavy cream and buttermilk in a glass or ceramic bowl. Cover with a clean kitchen towel and set aside at room temperature for 24 to 36 hours, or until the mixture thickens. After fermentation, refrigerate the mixture for 2 to 3 hours.

2 Pour the chilled mixture into the bowl of a stand mixer. Whip with the whisk attachment on high speed for 3 to 5 minutes, or until the cream breaks down into small curds resembling a very yellow cottage cheese. You will also see the buttermilk separating from the cream. (Alternatively, you can do this by shaking the mixture in a lidded glass jar until you achieve the same result, but this takes time and elbow grease!)

3 Line a strainer with a double layer of cheesecloth, position over a medium bowl, and pour the curdled cream into it. The buttermilk will run through. Gather the cheesecloth with clean hands and tightly squeeze out any remaining buttermilk. I like to leave it over the bowl for a while longer until the butter is well strained. The resulting buttermilk can be used in baking or even salad dressings or marinades.

4 Transfer the butter to a bowl and season with the salt, incorporating it with a wooden spoon or fork. Place the butter in the center of a piece of parchment paper, and roll the sides to shape it into a log. Wrap tightly and refrigerate. The butter will keep for several weeks.

Crème Fraîche

2 cups (450 ml) heavy cream
¼ cup (55 ml) cultured
  buttermilk or whole-milk
  yogurt (page 32)

Note: Look for the richest heavy cream you can find, preferably unhomogenized and with 36 to 40 percent fat content.

Crème fraîche is essentially cultured heavy cream. Thick, creamy, and tangy, it elevates so many dishes where an extra acidity is needed that heavy cream alone might not deliver. I love crème fraîche atop sweet summer fruits or swirled into a creamy root vegetable puree.

To speed up the fermentation process, the cream should stay at around 75 degrees F, so in the cooler winter months, you might want to place the mixture in the oven with the oven light on. You could also use a yogurt maker for this. In warmer months, you can simply leave the cream at room temperature.

MAKES 2 CUPS

1   Combine the heavy cream and buttermilk in a quart jar with an airtight lid. Seal and give the jar a good shake to mix thoroughly. Remove the lid, cover the jar with cheesecloth secured with a rubber band, and set aside at room temperature for 12 to 24 hours, until the cream thickens.

2   Remove the cheesecloth, reseal with the lid, and refrigerate for at least 2 hours The crème fraîche will keep in the refrigerator for up to 1 week.

Simple Nut or Seed Butter

The possibilities are endless here: you can mix and match nuts, seeds, sweeteners, oils, and flavorings. I am keeping this recipe as simple as it gets so you can play around at home. My preference is for a butter that uses roasted nuts or seeds, is hardly sweetened, and has a bit of coconut oil and a pinch of sea salt. The fewer add-ons it contains, the longer it will last in the refrigerator.

MAKES 1¼ CUPS

2¼ cups (about 300 g) raw nuts or seeds (cashews, almonds, hazelnuts, pistachios, sunflower seeds)

3 to 4 tablespoons oil (melted coconut, chia seed, almond, flaxseed, grapeseed, olive, sesame, sunflower)

2 teaspoons coconut sugar, honey, or maple syrup (optional)

½ teaspoon flaky sea salt

Note: A high-speed blender will make the grinding so much faster. A food processor should also do the work, but it might take longer and the motor could overheat.

1   Preheat the oven to 300 degrees F. It's best to roast nuts and seeds at a lower temperature so they toast all the way through without burning. Place the nuts or seeds (or mix of both) on a baking sheet and roast for 15 minutes, or until slightly brown and fragrant.

2   Transfer to a high-speed blender or food processor and blend until the nuts are pulverized. You may need to stop and scrape the sides a few times until the consistency is even and resembles brown sugar. It will take a few minutes to pulverize the nuts; exactly how long depends on your machine. If the motor gets hot, stop and restart a few minutes later.

3   With the blender running, drizzle in 3 tablespoons of the oil and process until smooth, stopping halfway through to scrape the sides. Add a little more oil if needed, but let the blender do its work to fully incorporate the oil before adding too much. Add the sweetener and sea salt and mix until well combined.

4   Transfer the butter into a glass jar with an airtight lid, seal, and store in the refrigerator for up to 1 month.

Chocolate-Hazelnut Butter

2 cups (300 g) raw hazelnuts
3 ounces (85 g) bittersweet
   chocolate, chopped
2 tablespoons melted coconut oil
1 tablespoon maple syrup
1 teaspoon vanilla extract
½ teaspoon flaky sea salt

This is my one exception to basic, lightly sweetened nut or seed butters. When it comes to this chocolate-hazelnut version, I go all the way into dessert territory, trying to mimic the Nutella of my youth. I love to spread it on Buckwheat Crêpes (page 92) or on toasted Nordic Rye-Style Seed Bread (page 101).

MAKES 1½ CUPS

1   Preheat the oven to 300 degrees F. Spread the hazelnuts on a baking sheet and bake for 15 minutes, or until fragrant. Transfer the hazelnuts to a clean kitchen towel and rub them together to peel off the skins. It's OK if you cannot remove them completely, but try to get as much as you can, as the skin is bitter.

2   Transfer the hazelnuts to a high-speed blender or food processor and blend until creamy, stopping to scrape the bowl a few times. It will take a few minutes to pulverize the hazelnuts; exactly how long depends on your machine. If the motor gets hot, stop and restart a few minutes later.

3   Meanwhile, bring a small pot with 2 inches of water to a simmer. Place the chocolate in a heatproof bowl and position over the pot. Reduce the heat to low and melt the chocolate, making sure no water gets into the bowl and no flames reach the sides. Add the melted chocolate to the blender and process until smooth and incorporated. Add the coconut oil, maple syrup, vanilla, and salt and blend until combined.

4   Transfer the butter to a glass jar with an airtight lid, seal, and store at room temperature for 2 weeks or in the refrigerator for up to 1 month. It will harden solid when refrigerated, so bring the butter to room temperature a couple of hours before using.

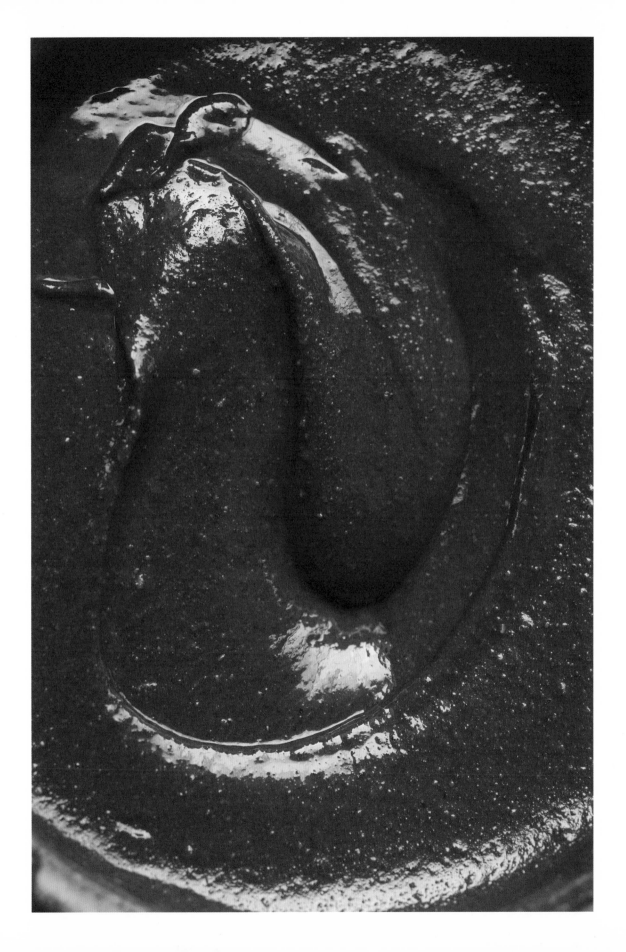

Whole-Milk Yogurt

3½ cups (790 g) whole milk (preferably with cream on top)
½ cup (115 g) cultured whole-milk yogurt, or the contents of 2 probiotic capsules (50 billion CPU)

Note: My preference is for full-fat milk that is unhomogenized and has the cream on top, but this isn't essential. You can even add ½ cup heavy cream for a richer yogurt. For the bacteria, I use probiotic powder (usually available in capsules at health-food stores), but you can use plain cultured yogurt that does not contain any thickeners for fermentation instead.

My father gifted my mother a yogurt maker sometime in the mid-1980s. I remember it clearly because my mother despised kitchen appliances, yet this bulky orange contraption sat on our counter for years. As you might imagine, we ate a lot of homemade yogurt. It was never sweetened and was always made with whole milk that came up from the same dairy that provided it for the pastry shop.

I encourage you to make your own yogurt at home and stay away from the highly sweetened and artificially thickened commercial varieties. It is simple, delicious, and good for your gut.

MAKES 1 QUART

1   Heat the milk in a medium pot over low heat until it reaches 110 degrees F. If it exceeds 110 degrees F, let the milk cool, because higher temperatures might kill the bacteria. Ladle ½ cup of the warm milk into a bowl, and whisk in the yogurt. Pour this mixture back into the pot and stir until well combined.

2   Pour the mixture into eight (4-ounce) glass jars. (Note that any size jars can be used, even a large 1-quart glass container). Set the jars on a baking sheet and place in the oven, uncovered, with the oven light on for 8 to 12 hours. Cover with lids and chill in the refrigerator for at least 2 hours before serving. The yogurt will keep, refrigerated, for up to 1 week.

Mayonnaise

1 raw egg yolk, at room
   temperature
2 teaspoons freshly squeezed
   lemon juice
1 teaspoon Dijon mustard
1 teaspoon water
½ teaspoon kosher salt
¾ cup extra-virgin olive oil

Note: I love an all–olive oil
mayonnaise, but I realize that
might be too intense for many.
If that is the case, you can
replace some or all the olive oil
with a more neutral-tasting oil,
such as safflower.

I didn't even know that jarred mayonnaise existed until I began
eating at friends' houses. My grandmother and mother always
made mayonnaise to order. Nearly every Sunday, as many
Basque families do, we started our lunch with white asparagus
or Russian salad. Both are served with a generous side of
mayonnaise, and it was my job to help prepare it. We used an
old immersion blender and a tall, clear plastic cup to emulsify
the egg and oil. At my grandmother's command, I poured the oil
in a slow, steady drizzle as she moved the immersion blender
up and down. It was precise. The mayonnaise would be served
immediately after, then leftovers discarded.

    Yes, this recipe calls for raw egg. Yes, there is always a risk for
salmonella, so I recommend you use the freshest eggs available
and wash your egg thoroughly right before cracking it open to
wash off any harmful bacteria. I still deem it a delicious pleasure.

MAKES 1 CUP

1 Combine the egg yolk, lemon juice, mustard, water, and salt
in a blender. Add 1 tablespoon of the oil and blend until smooth.
In a slow, steady stream, continue adding the remaining oil
with the blender running. It will become thick and creamy. Use
immediately. You may refrigerate leftovers for up to a day, but
I recommend using it right away.

Flavoring Mayonnaise

I love taking the basic mayonnaise recipe and flavoring it to suit different dishes I'm making. Here are some ideas.

Aioli

Follow the basic recipe but mash 2 cloves garlic with the salt in a mortar and pestle first. Proceed as directed. Serve with fries, roasted vegetables, or leftover roasted chicken.

Roasted Garlic Aioli

Cut a head of garlic crosswise. Place it on a baking sheet and drizzle the cut tops with 1 teaspoon olive oil. Bake at 400 degrees F for about 45 minutes, or until golden brown. The garlic will smell sweet and caramelized. Cool slightly, then squeeze the tender cloves into a bowl and mash them with a fork. Prepare the basic mayonnaise recipe, and stir it into the mashed garlic. It's perfect slathered on meat sandwiches or roasted potatoes.

Flower and Herb

Prepare the basic mayonnaise recipe and fold ¼ cup finely chopped herbs and flowers into it. Some of my favorites are chives, basil, lemon balm, marigold petals, dandelion petals, chickweed, and watercress. It pairs nicely with grilled fish, roasted vegetables, and summer tomato sandwiches.

Hot and Spicy

Prepare the basic mayonnaise recipe and stir in 2 tablespoons sriracha, chili oil, or other spicy condiment. This is my favorite for a snack of hard-cooked eggs or a leftover roasted chicken sandwich.

Seedy

Read about collecting your own seeds on page 38. Toast 2 teaspoons of the seeds, such as fennel, parsley, cumin, or coriander, in a skillet over low heat until fragrant, then grind with a mortar and pestle. Prepare the basic mayonnaise recipe and stir in the seeds.

Labneh

---

3 cups (675 g) whole-milk yogurt
   (page 32)
1 clove garlic, finely minced
½ teaspoon freshly squeezed
   lemon juice
½ teaspoon flaky sea salt
1 teaspoon za'atar
2 tablespoons extra-virgin
   olive oil

My friend Mayssam, who grew up in Lebanon, introduced me to *labneh* when I visited her in Montreal a few years ago. She spoke about labneh with a contagious sense of longing that I could relate to—the power of nostalgia in childhood food memories.

Labneh, in its simplest form, is strained yogurt that is seasoned with lemon and salt and then drizzled with olive oil, but you can always add other herbs and spices. Its consistency is that of spreadable cheese, and that's why it's often called yogurt cheese. Be sure to use whole-milk yogurt or—even better—make your own.

MAKES 2 CUPS

1   Line a strainer with cheesecloth and position over a medium bowl. Pour the yogurt into it, transfer the bowl to the refrigerator, and let the yogurt drain for 24 to 72 hours. After 24 hours, the labneh will be creamy and thick; at 72 hours it will have the consistency of spreadable cheese. I like it somewhere in between.

2   Transfer the labneh to a bowl and stir in the garlic, lemon juice, and salt. Sprinkle the top with za'atar and drizzle with olive oil. Store covered in the refrigerator for up to 7 days.

Drying Herbs and Collecting Seeds

I have a vegetable garden in my backyard. Not so big that we can live off our harvest, but big enough that I can plant some herbs and vegetables to introduce variety to my meals during the summer months. I also collect herb flowers for my home. They live in vases for a bit, and when they begin to wilt, I tie them in string and hang them upside down all over the house. It's the best way to dry them, but they also make my home feel special, decorated for no particular holiday. When I visit the farmers' market, I look for the more unusual herbs that are challenging to come by at the supermarket. I'll collect these and dry them to use throughout the year.

Drying Herbs

1 Gently wash herbs in cold water, and remove any dead leaves or stems. Lay the herbs on paper towels and gently pat them dry.

2 Gather a small bunch of herbs at a time so all the stems can be exposed to air and dry evenly. Wrap twine around the bottoms of the stems, leaving a length of twine that can be used for hanging.

3 Hang the bunches of herbs upside down. I might hammer a nail into the wall and wrap the twine around it, or use a strip of tape to secure it instead. Let the herbs dry completely as any moisture could cause mold to grow.

4 Once completely dry, transfer the herbs to a jar with an airtight lid, and seal. The herbs will keep for months. Note that drying herbs concentrates their flavor; the general rule is to use about a third of the amount of fresh herbs.

Drying Seeds and Blossoms

1 Wait until seed flowers in the garden are turning slightly brown, then harvest by clipping the flower stems.

2 As with herbs, gather small bunches of the stems and wrap them with twine. Hang upside down and allow to dry completely.

3 Once dry, lay parchment paper on a work surface and shake the seeds from the flower heads; they should come right off. Transfer the seeds to a glass jar with an airtight lid, and seal. They will keep for months.

Dukkah

¾ cup (120 g) raw hazelnuts, almonds, pistachios, or other nut of choice
⅓ cup (55 g) hulled sesame seeds
2 tablespoons cumin seeds
2 tablespoons coriander seeds
1 tablespoon fennel seeds
2 teaspoons dried rose or other flower petals (optional)
2 teaspoons flaky sea salt
1½ teaspoons freshly ground black pepper

I first encountered *dukkah* during one of my many early morning breakfast meetings at Seattle's London Plane. Soft-cooked eggs sprinkled with rose and hazelnut dukkah were my usual until they stopped serving it. I went home and decided to create my own version of the spice blend.

Dukkah, an Egyptian spice blend, has become quite trendy in recent years. I use this mixture of seeds and nuts simply: on eggs, salads, roasted vegetables, and fish. It adds so much crunch and texture to dishes that I reference this recipe throughout the book.

MAKES APPROXIMATELY 1 CUP

1 Preheat the oven to 325 degrees F. Spread the nuts on a baking sheet and roast until fragrant, about 15 minutes. Place them in a clean kitchen towel and rub them together to loosen the skins. Discard the skins. Chop the nuts coarsely and transfer to a medium bowl.

2 Toast the sesame seeds in a dry skillet over medium heat until lightly golden and fragrant, about 1 minute. Add them to the bowl with the nuts. Toast the cumin, coriander, and fennel seeds in the same skillet until fragrant, about another minute. Transfer to a mortar and pestle and grind coarsely. Alternatively, you can use a spice grinder for a finer grind.

3 Transfer the ground seeds to the bowl and add the rose petals, salt, and pepper. Stir well. Dukkah can be stored in a sealed jar for up to 1 month.

Mix-and-Match Granola

3 cups (about 260 g) gluten-free
    grains
1½ cups (about 225 g) nuts
    and seeds
½ cup (115 g) fruit juice
½ cup (115 g) liquid sweetener
¼ cup (55 g) oil
1 tablespoon vanilla extract
1 teaspoon flaky sea salt
½ teaspoon ground spices
1½ cups (170 g) dried fruit

There are so many combinations of granola on the market shelves these days. Here, I've simplified the ingredient ratios and amounts so you can mix and match and create your own blend. Oats make up the majority of my base, but sometimes I incorporate quinoa flakes or buckwheat groats depending on the flavor I want to achieve.

MAKES 6 CUPS

1 Preheat the oven to 300 degrees F. Combine the grains, nuts, and seeds in a large bowl. Combine the juice, sweetener, oil, vanilla, salt, and spices in a medium bowl. Pour the wet ingredients over the dry and toss to coat. Spread the mixture evenly on a large baking sheet. Bake, stirring the mixture about every 15 minutes, for 40 to 50 minutes total, or until evenly golden.

2 Let the granola cool completely in the pan. It will become crunchier as it sits. Stir in the dried fruit. Store in an airtight container at room temperature for up to 1 month. Note that if you are using butter in the granola, it should be consumed within 5 days.

GRAINS: rolled oats, buckwheat groats, quinoa flakes

NUTS AND SEEDS: pecans, coconut flakes, walnuts, cashews, peanuts, almonds, hazelnuts, pistachios, pepitas, poppy seeds, sunflower seeds, flaxseeds, chia seeds

FRUIT JUICE: apple juice, orange juice, pineapple juice

LIQUID SWEETENER: maple syrup, honey

OIL: coconut oil, olive oil, almond oil, flaxseed oil, melted butter, browned butter

SPICES: cinnamon, nutmeg, ginger, cardamom, mace, allspice

DRIED FRUIT: cranberries, cherries, raisins, apricots, figs, raspberries, strawberries, blueberries, mango, pineapple, currants, apples

Pickled Vegetables

1 pound (454 g) assorted fresh
  vegetables, sliced
2 cups (450 g) vinegar
1 cup (225 g) filtered water
½ cup (100 g) sugar
2 tablespoons whole spices
1 tablespoon kosher salt

The first time I traveled to Sweden I came home with a case of Perstorp Attika 24 percent acetic vinegar. I was told it's what everyone in Sweden uses to make their quick-pickle brines, and the bottle had a very simple ratio recipe that I've been using ever since. This brine is slightly sweet, so you can reduce the amount of sugar if desired.

When it comes to the type of vinegar, I like anything that's not too dark. White distilled and apple cider vinegars are my preference. Then there is a whole world of flavor you can add through spices: bay leaves, various peppercorns and dried chilies, cumin and coriander seeds, star anise, and more.

This recipe makes a lot of pickles, so you can easily halve or even quarter it, but I always make good use of a full batch. You will see that many of the recipes in this book refer back to this page.

MAKES TWO 1-QUART JARS

1 Clean two quart jars with lids in hot soapy water and dry well. Divide the vegetables among the jars.

2 Combine the vinegar, water, sugar, spices, and salt in a medium saucepan over high heat and bring to a boil. Reduce the heat and simmer, stirring occasionally, until the sugar dissolves. Pour the brine into the jars, and press the vegetables down with a wooden spoon to pack them in.

3 Let the vegetables sit at room temperature for about 30 minutes, or until cool. The brine will begin to discolor the vegetables. Seal the jars and refrigerate the pickles for at least 2 hours before using. They will keep in the refrigerator for up to 1 week.

FLAVOR COMBINATIONS

Radish + bay leaf + peppercorns

Shallot + bay leaf + crushed garlic + thyme + peppercorns

Fennel + red onion + orange zest + fennel seeds + vanilla bean

Green tomato + star anise + chile de árbol

Cucumber + crushed garlic + dill flower and seeds
  + red pepper flakes

Whole baby carrots + peeled sliced ginger + cumin seeds

Shrubs and Drinking Vinegars

2 cups (450 g) diced fruit
1 to 2 cups (200 g to 400 g) sugar
2 cups (450 g) vinegar

A shrub is essentially a fruit syrup made by macerating fruit and sugar that is then mixed with vinegar. It's really easy to remember the recipe—an equal ratio in volume of fruit, sugar, and vinegar. In general, I like to make mine pungent and add a little bit less sugar when using fruit that is naturally very sweet, but keeping this ratio in mind will always be a good guideline. This is a perfect way to use up overripe fruit that has started to ferment slightly. Play with different vinegars to complement different fruits.

MAKES 3 CUPS

1   Combine the fruit and sugar in a glass or ceramic bowl. Toss to combine and lightly bruise the fruit with a wooden spoon so it releases a bit of juice and kickstarts maceration. Cover the bowl with plastic wrap and set aside at room temperature for 24 hours. The sugar will extract the natural fruit juices and melt into the liquid.

2   After 24 hours, stir the mixture again, which should be syrupy. Pour in the vinegar and stir to combine. Cover the bowl again and set aside to macerate at room temperature for another 24 hours.

3   Transfer the bowl to the refrigerator and leave there for 7 more days.

4   Strain the syrup through a fine-mesh sieve into a glass jar with an airtight lid. Discard the fruit. The shrub can be served with sparkling water or in any cocktail of your choice. It will keep in the fridge for up to 1 month.

FLAVOR COMBINATIONS

Peach + cardamom + thyme + champagne vinegar

Pear + fresh grated ginger + apple cider vinegar

Strawberry + rhubarb + pink peppercorns + red wine vinegar

Plum + star anise + rice vinegar

Persimmon + cardamom + fresh grated ginger + apple cider vinegar

Apple + spruce tips + vanilla bean + apple cider vinegar

Preserved Lemons

---

8 to 10 lemons (about 2 pounds
   or 1 kg), some of which will be
   for juicing
Coarse sea salt or kosher salt
1 bay leaf
4 black peppercorns
Extra-virgin olive oil

Preserved lemons have found a place in contemporary cooking, but the floral brininess of their cured flesh has been a staple in many Middle Eastern and African cuisines for centuries. I didn't grow up with preserved citrus on hand, even though southern Spain has a legacy of Moorish cooking; nowadays, however, jarred lemons are always in my pantry. Every winter, when citrus is abundant, I make time to preserve cases of them.

I only cure citrus that is organic, unwaxed, and has beautiful thin skin—Meyer lemons are ideal because they are naturally very fragrant. I have also cured other citrus, such as grapefruit, mandarins, and oranges. The juice of these sweeter fruits is not acidic enough to cure them properly, so I supplement it with lemon juice. Citrus fruit can be left whole, sliced, or quartered (with or without ends attached). I have tried them all and the results are similar; however, the curing time will be shorter when the fruit is thinly sliced.

Using the right salt is nearly as important. I prefer coarse sea salt and stay away from processed table salt. I don't follow an exact amount—the more the merrier in this case. All the cut edges and layers of the fruit should be rubbed with abundant salt for best results. You can add herbs and spices to the jar as well, but I like to keep my seasonings very simple: a bay leaf and a few peppercorns.

MAKES 1 QUART

1 Wash the lemons thoroughly and dry them.

2 Cut six of the lemons into quarters or slices. Rub the cut edges with abundant sea salt. I do this over a bowl to collect the salt that falls off and reduce the mess.

3   Sprinkle 2 to 3 tablespoons salt in the bottom of a quart jar with an airtight lid. Press the cut lemons tightly into the jar, layering more salt in between them. Push down on the lemons to squeeze out their juices—I like to use the bottom of a small jar or ramekin to help with this. Leave some space at the top of the jar and fill with additional lemon juice (from the remaining lemons) until the fruit is fully submerged—this is very important. Add the bay leaf and peppercorns. Seal the jar and set aside in a dark, cool place for 4 weeks.

4   Shake the jar every day for 2 weeks to distribute the salt and juice. After this time, open the jar and pour in enough olive oil to cover the top. This will help protect the lemons from bacteria. Return the jar to a dark cool place for 2 more weeks or longer (during which you don't need to shake the jar). The preserved lemons are ready when the flesh is tender. If you can wait, leave them for 3 months for extra floral, tender goodness. They can be stored, covered, at room temperature for up to a year. When you remove a preserved lemon from the jar, add more salt and lemon juice to keep the remaining lemons covered. Rinse the cured fruit with water before using.

Chicken Stock

4 pounds (1.4 kg) raw chicken bones (necks, wings, feet)
2 medium yellow onions, peeled and quartered
2 medium carrots, scrubbed and halved
2 medium stalks celery, halved
4 sprigs Italian parsley
1 tablespoon kosher salt
5 black peppercorns

I make large batches of chicken stock at home, then freeze it in quart containers. There are two methods I use: one uses raw bones and the other, a leftover roasted chicken carcass. The flavor profile and color of the two are quite different, so which you choose depends how you like to use stock. The raw bones will result in a clearer, lighter broth, as opposed to the smokier, darker roasted bone broth.

If you can find chicken feet, I highly recommend using them. They are full of natural gelatin, which is great for your health and also makes for a very rich, viscous broth. I buy feet at the farmers' market in large bags (usually frozen).

You can make stock in a large pot on the stove or in a pressure cooker to save time. I find the pressure cooker results in a clearer and more flavorful broth, plus it is so much faster, but both methods work. This recipe uses the stovetop method. If you elect to use a pressure cooker, follow the manufacturer's instructions for timing, but the ingredient measures are the same.

MAKES ABOUT 4 QUARTS

1   Combine all the ingredients in a large stockpot and add about 6 quarts cold water, or enough to cover by 2 inches. Bring the water to a boil over high heat, then reduce to a simmer.

2   Simmer, uncovered, for 2 hours, skimming off any impurities that rise to the surface. (If using a pressure cooker, there will be hardly any impurities in the broth afterward.)

3   Strain the stock through a fine-mesh sieve into quart glass jars. Cool completely at room temperature. Refrigerate for up to 1 week or freeze for up to 3 months.

Beef Stock

5 pounds (2.3 kg) beef bones,
  preferably with lots of marrow
  exposed (oxtail and knuckle)
1 pound (455 g) beef short ribs
2 medium yellow onions, peeled
  and quartered
2 medium carrots, scrubbed
  and halved
2 medium stalks celery, halved
1 tablespoon apple cider vinegar
1 tablespoon kosher salt
4 sprigs Italian parsley
1 bay leaf
10 black peppercorns

Beef stock is definitely an all-day event when making it on the stovetop. When I was a pastry chef, the adjacent banquet kitchen always had an enormous stockpot full of beef bones and all kinds of vegetable scraps that simmered for what seemed like days. Mostly I have been using my electric pressure cooker to make stocks these days, but this recipe is for the stovetop method.

MAKES ABOUT 4 QUARTS

1   Preheat the oven to 400 degrees F. Rinse the beef bones in cold water, then pat them dry with paper towels. Toss the bones, short ribs, onions, carrots, and celery on a large baking sheet and bake for about 45 minutes, stirring all the ingredients halfway through, or until the bones and vegetables are slightly caramelized.

2   Transfer everything from the pan to a large stockpot with the vinegar, salt, parsley, bay leaf, and peppercorns. Add about 6 quarts cold water, or enough to cover by 2 inches. Bring the water to a boil over high heat, then reduce to a simmer, skimming off any impurities that rise to the surface.

3   Simmer, uncovered, for 8 to 10 hours, making sure the water never boils. Strain the stock through a fine-mesh sieve into quart glass jars. Cool completely at room temperature. Refrigerate for up to 1 week or freeze for up to 3 months. Note that once the stock has chilled, the fat will solidify on the surface. I skim a lot of the fat off before using the stock.

Fish Stock

_____

4 pounds (1.8 kg) fish bones
  and heads
1 yellow onion, cut into ½-inch
  dice
1 medium carrot, scrubbed and
  cut into ½-inch dice
1 medium stalk celery, cut into
  ½-inch dice

When I moved to the US, I noticed that most people didn't really know what to do with fish heads and buying whole fish seemed to be more complicated than back home. I encourage you to purchase whole fish whenever you can and have your fishmonger prep it for you. Keep the fillets but also ask for the heads, skin, and bones, because they make the best fish stock you can use for soups.

MAKES ABOUT 6 CUPS

1 Rinse the fish bones and heads in cold water. Place them in a large stockpot with the onion, carrot, celery, and 10 cups cold water. Bring the water to a boil over medium-high heat, then reduce to a simmer, skimming off any impurities and foam that rise to the surface. Simmer, uncovered, for 20 minutes.

2 Remove the pot from the heat and cover with plastic wrap. Cool completely at room temperature without disturbing the pot. This will help create a richly flavored clear stock.

3 Strain the stock through a fine-mesh sieve into quart glass containers. Refrigerate for up to 1 week or freeze for up to 3 months.

Vegetable Stock

---

2 tablespoons extra-virgin
  olive oil
3 medium skin-on yellow onions,
  cut into 1-inch dice
8 stalks celery, cut into
  1-inch dice
3 medium carrots, cut into
  1-inch dice
12 ounces (340 g) cremini
  mushrooms
1 medium leek, cut into
  1-inch dice
1 medium fennel, cut into
  1-inch dice
1 large head garlic, cut crosswise
5 sprigs Italian parsley
5 sprigs thyme
1 bay leaf
5 black peppercorns
1 (4-inch) piece kombu (optional)
1 tablespoon kosher salt

Making vegetable stock is a perfect way to use up the vegetable scraps that accumulate throughout the day—onion skins, carrot peels, mushroom bottoms, celery ends, fennel fronds, and more. Freeze the scraps in a ziplock bag until you have enough for a batch of stock—you will need about 2 cups vegetable scraps per quart of water. Note that not all vegetables are well suited for stock. Avoid very starchy ones, such as russet potatoes, because they will cloud the broth and make it a bit gummy. Bitter greens can be overpowering, and beets will add too much of an earthy taste as well as stain the liquid.

If you don't have any scraps on hand, or need to supplement what you do, follow this recipe for a flavorful, well-balanced stock.

MAKES ABOUT 3 QUARTS

1 Heat the oil in a large stockpot over medium-high heat. Add the rest of the ingredients and stir to combine. Cook the vegetables, stirring occasionally, until they begin to soften and brown slightly, about 10 minutes.

2 Add about 6 quarts cold water, or enough to cover by 2 inches. Bring the water to a boil over high heat, then reduce to a simmer.

3 Simmer for about 1 hour, or until the liquid has reduced by half. Strain the stock through a fine-mesh sieve into quart glass jars. Cool completely at room temperature. Refrigerate for up to 1 week or freeze for up to 3 months.

Gluten-Free Sourdough Starter

My sourdough starter is three years old and it keeps on giving. It was inspired by Naomi Devlin's book *River Cottage Gluten Free*. That cookbook and Naomi's personal blog narrate her own sourdough journey, and both are great resources for anyone looking for answers.

Creating your own starter only requires flour, water, wild yeast, and time. It is simple, but there are a few things to consider. My favorite flour to use is superfine brown rice flour, because it is mild in flavor and suitable for many different recipes. You can also make a starter with teff, buckwheat, millet, or quinoa flours, but I find brown rice is easiest. Do not attempt to make a starter using only white rice flour—the white rice has been stripped of the germ, which is essential to the process. Do not use tap water because any traces of chlorine will kill yeast and bacteria. It is best to use either filtered tap water (my preference) or bottled water.

Trouble-shooting

1 If the starter is not bubbly after 4 days, try stirring in 1 tablespoon plain active yogurt or kefir. The cultures in the yogurt can help boost fermentation.

2 If the starter is not bubbly after 4 days, the room might be too cool—make sure it's in the temperature range of 70 to 75 degrees F. You can help the starter by placing the bowl in a lukewarm water bath for a few hours.

3 Yeast loves a little bit of sugar as food, so if the starter isn't growing, add some unwashed grapes or a little freshly squeezed pear juice to the starter to help it ferment.

4 I notice that my filtered tap water is very cold in the winter compared to summer, so I usually warm it up in a pot or kettle to about 70 degrees F—but no hotter or it could kill the yeast. Never use hot tap water.

5 After the starter is established and being kept in the refrigerator, it can develop a grayish liquid on top. This is normal. Pour this liquid out before using.

1 cup (140 g) superfine brown
  rice flour
¾ cup plus 2 tablespoons
  (190 g) filtered water, at
  room temperature

DAY 1

In a medium ceramic or glass bowl, whisk together the flour and water until it forms a paste. Cover the bowl with a clean linen towel or a plate and set aside at room temperature for 24 hours. Ideally the room should be between 70 and 75 degrees F.

⅓ cup (45 g) superfine brown
  rice flour
¼ cup (60 g) filtered water, at
  room temperature

DAY 2

Whisk the starter. Add the flour and water and whisk to combine. Cover again and set aside for another 24 hours at room temperature.

⅓ cup (45 g) superfine brown
  rice flour
¼ cup (60 g) filtered water, at
  room temperature

DAY 3

By now the mixture should start bubbling up slightly and smell sour, like yogurt. Whisk the starter. Add the flour and water, whisk, cover, and set aside for another 24 hours at room temperature.

⅓ cup (45 g) superfine brown
  rice flour
¼ cup (60 g) filtered water, at
  room temperature

DAY 4

Once again, whisk the starter. Whisk in the flour and water, cover, and set aside for another 24 hours at room temperature.

1 cup (140 g) superfine brown
  rice flour
¾ cup plus 2 tablespoons
  (190 g) filtered water, at
  room temperature

DAY 5

The starter should be bubbly now and is nearly ready to use. Whisk the starter, then add in the flour and water and transfer to a 2-quart glass container with an airtight lid. Let the starter ferment, uncovered, at room temperature for 24 hours. The starter is now ready, but if you're not going to use it right away, seal the jar and store in the refrigerator.

Using and Feeding Sourdough Starter

All recipes in this book that call for sourdough starter should begin with cold starter straight from the refrigerator.

When you are ready to proceed with a recipe, stir the entire starter, measure out the amount of cold starter the recipe calls for, and then transfer the remaining starter to a large bowl. Proceed with the cold starter as directed by the recipe. The remaining starter needs to be fed.

Feed the starter 1 cup (140 g) of superfine brown rice flour and ¾ cup plus 2 tablespoons (190 g) room-temperature filtered water and whisk together until smooth. Transfer the starter into a clean glass jar with an airtight lid, then set aside, uncovered, at room temperature for 4 to 5 hours, or until bubbly. Once the starter bubbles up again, seal the jar and return it to the refrigerator until next use. The starter will likely deflate in the refrigerator, which is completely normal.

It is best to use the sourdough starter twice a week as it forces you to feed it regularly. However, the starter will be fine and healthy in the refrigerator for up to 1 week. If you don't plan to make anything with it within a week, remove and discard about 1 cup of the starter and feed the remainder as instructed above.

If you will be away for more than a week, I recommend asking a friend to take over feeding duty for you. It will save you having to start over or making a lot of adjustments later as starters can become too acidic if not fed and used regularly.

CHAPTER TWO

Morning

As a steadfast morning person and mother of two, I revel in the quiet hours before the sun rises. This is the time to be fully in my body, to set my intention for the day. I usually wake up before anyone else in my family. Before thinking of coffee or breakfast, I begin with a short meditation, bringing focus and positive energy into myself. While I'm a basic practitioner of meditation, that subtle shift in energy is necessary to treat myself with the utmost care throughout the day. When I allow for this space, I find that my decisions are made more consciously, particularly as I make my way into the kitchen. An homage to my mother, I start with half a cup of warm water, a splash of apple cider vinegar, and a drizzle of honey. My mother claims this morning ritual helps support digestion and therefore immunity—so I follow along.

I believe that when we put food into our bodies, our state of being is as much a part of that consumption as the tasting, the chewing, the swallowing. I believe that fear or anxiety can be consumed right along with the food, so I choose to be mindful and ingest my food in a more positive state. While you might not identify as a morning person, create time to develop your own ritual. At least try to allow for the mental space to make a positive, mindful decision about what you put in your body each morning.

Weekday mornings have a certain beat and timing. Breakfast must be simple, fairly quick, and nutritious to get us going on our busy schedules. Soft-cooked eggs with bitter greens and dukkah (something I always have on hand) on toast, or maybe a spicy shot of juice made with carrot, grapefruit, and sunflower butter. Or my children's favorite: egg tostadas with fennel and radish. Weekends allow us to linger and indulge in sourdough waffles with carmelized peaches, or buckwheat crêpes with chocolate-hazelnut butter. The recipes in this chapter begin with quicker weekday options and end with my family's weekend favorites.

Ginger-Turmeric Milk

3 cups (675 g) almond milk
    (page 20) or coconut milk
    (page 21)
3 tablespoons freshly grated
    turmeric, or 1½ teaspoons
    ground
2 tablespoons freshly grated
    ginger, or 1 teaspoon ground
2 tablespoons dried chamomile
    flowers or loose herbal tea
1 tablespoon coconut oil
1 to 2 tablespoons honey
    (preferably raw and local)
1 cinnamon stick
1 vanilla bean, split lengthwise
    and seeds scraped
4 black peppercorns
3 green cardamom pods,
    cracked
⅛ teaspoon kosher salt
1 teaspoon ground cinnamon,
    for sprinkling

I was introduced to the concept of "golden milk" by my friend Tara O'Brady, author of *Seven Spoons*, who grew up with the delicious treat thanks to the rich tradition of her Indian heritage. This is my own interpretation of the steeped milk that has become quite a sensation in the last few years (and I see why). It is delicious and full of anti-inflammatory properties from the turmeric, ginger, and cinnamon. If you prefer a creamier version, you could use canned coconut milk, which tends to be thicker than homemade.

MAKES 3 CUPS

1 Combine everything but the ground cinnamon in a medium saucepan over low heat. Simmer for 10 minutes.

2 Strain the milk through layers of cheesecloth into a glass jar and serve hot with a dash of ground cinnamon. The milk can be stored in a sealed glass jar for up to 3 days in the refrigerator. It may separate, so give it a good shake before reheating.

Spicy Carrot-Grapefruit Juice

In general, I don't enjoy sweet juices or smoothies in the morning. But add a little bit of spice or acidity—even vinegar—to a fruit juice, and I am all for it. If you don't have a juicer, use ½ cup each carrot and grapefruit juices and grate ½ teaspoon each fresh turmeric and ginger. Stir together and proceed with the second instruction.

MAKES 1 CUP

1 Press the carrots, grapefruit, turmeric, and ginger through a juicer.

2 Combine the juice, sunflower butter, honey, cayenne, and cinnamon in a high-speed blender and blend until frothy. Serve in a chilled glass and drink immediately.

3 medium carrots
1 grapefruit, peeled and halved
1 (½-inch piece) turmeric
1 (½-inch piece) ginger
1 tablespoon sunflower seed
  butter or almond butter
  (page 28)
½ teaspoon honey (preferably
  raw and local)
⅛ teaspoon cayenne
⅛ teaspoon ground cinnamon

Turmeric Detox Broth with Swiss Chard

2 tablespoons extra-virgin olive oil

6 cloves garlic, minced

1 yellow onion, diced

3 tablespoons grated turmeric

2 tablespoons grated ginger

1 dried chile de árbol (optional)

1 tablespoon cumin seeds

1 tablespoon coriander seeds

1 teaspoon freshly ground black pepper

1 teaspoon kosher salt

6 cups (1.5 liters) chicken stock (page 53)

2 tablespoons apple cider vinegar

4 cups very finely chopped Swiss chard

I drink this invigorating broth in the morning throughout the year, and even in the afternoon as a tea in the colder months. It's relatively easy to make once you have good chicken stock in your fridge or freezer. When I'm planning to make this broth, I try to use chicken stock that had a lot of chicken feet in it because they are full of collagen—the stock sets like gelatin.

MAKES 6 SERVINGS

1   Heat a Dutch oven or stockpot over medium heat. Add the olive oil, garlic, and onion and cook until tender, about 5 minutes. Stir in the turmeric, ginger, chile de árbol, cumin, coriander, black pepper, and salt. Add the stock and vinegar and bring to a simmer. Reduce the heat to low, cover, and cook for 20 minutes. Strain the broth through a fine-mesh sieve. The broth can be stored in the refrigerator for up to 5 days.

2   Divide the Swiss chard among soup bowls or large mugs. Pour the hot broth over the chard and let steep for 5 minutes. Drink immediately.

Roasted Cherries with Coconut Granola

If you have never roasted cherries, I strongly encourage you to do so. Their flavor deepens with heat, and if you roast them whole, their pit imparts a subtle almond-like flavor. You could very well serve them for dessert over some vanilla ice cream.

MAKES 4 SERVINGS

1 Preheat the oven to 425 degrees F. Toss the cherries with the maple syrup, water, and salt and spread on a baking sheet. Bake for 10 to 15 minutes, or until the cherries burst and their juices create a light syrup. The roasted cherries can be eaten warm or stored in a jar in the refrigerator for up to 3 days.

2 Divide the yogurt among bowls and top with the granola, roasted cherries, and bee pollen.

1 pound (454 g) cherries, whole or pitted
1 tablespoon maple syrup
1 tablespoon water
¼ teaspoon kosher salt
2 cups (450 g) whole-milk yogurt (page 32)
2 cups (450 g) Coconut Granola (recipe follows)
2 tablespoons bee pollen (optional)

Coconut Granola

The combination of coconut, hazelnuts, and apricots is one of my favorites, and I keep it on hand at home for breakfast or snacks. It's also my go-to with roasted cherries and yogurt.

MAKES 6 CUPS

1 Preheat the oven to 300 degrees F. Combine the oats, coconut, and hazelnuts in a large bowl. Combine the maple syrup, orange juice, oil, vanilla, salt, and cinnamon in a medium bowl. Pour the wet ingredients over the dry and toss to coat. Spread the mixture evenly on a large baking sheet. Bake, stirring the mixture about every 15 minutes, for 40 to 50 minutes total, or until evenly golden.

2 Let the granola cool completely in the pan. It will become crunchier as it sits. Stir in the apricots. Store in an airtight container at room temperature for up to 1 month.

3 cups (260 g) gluten-free rolled oats
1 cup (80 g) packed coconut flakes
½ cup (75 g) raw hazelnuts, coarsely chopped
½ cup (140 g) maple syrup
½ cup (115 g) freshly squeezed orange juice
¼ cup (55 g) coconut oil
1 tablespoon vanilla extract
1 teaspoon flaky sea salt
½ teaspoon ground cinnamon
1½ cups (170 g) chopped dried apricots

Bircher Muesli with Poached Rhubarb and Hazelnuts

For the muesli
1½ cups (340 g) cashew milk
(page 20)
1 cup (100 g) gluten-free
rolled oats
½ cup (75 g) peeled grated apple
(about ½ medium apple)

For the poached rhubarb
8 ounces (225 g) rhubarb, cut
into 1½-inch slices
2 tablespoons water
1 tablespoon freshly squeezed
orange juice
1 tablespoon honey (preferably
raw and local)

For serving
½ cup (75 g) hazelnuts, toasted
and coarsely chopped

Bircher muesli is essentially a grain mixture that is soaked overnight in milk or juice and served with fruit. It can be such an easy, go-to breakfast when you're pressed for time. The beautiful thing about it is that you don't really need a recipe. Simply remember the ratios: one part grain to two parts liquid by volume.

The grain is traditionally oats, which is usually what I use. I have soaked buckwheat and quinoa flakes before, but oats retain the best texture. The liquid can be anything from milk to fruit juice, but there is one must: Bircher muesli shouldn't be without grated apple. I like my liquid to be 75 percent nut milk and 25 percent grated apple, which is not technically liquid but it has a lot of juice and sweetens the mixture. Beyond that, the world is your oyster.

Here is one of my favorite adaptations that I make in the first months of spring when rhubarb finally makes an appearance in our garden.

MAKES 2 SERVINGS

1 Make the muesli the day before serving. Mix together the milk, oats, and apple in a medium bowl. Cover with plastic wrap and refrigerate for at least 6 hours or overnight.

2 To make the poached rhubarb, place the rhubarb in a shallow saucepan big enough to fit it all in a single layer. This will help it cook evenly. Pour the water and orange juice into the pan. Drizzle the honey all over the rhubarb.

3 Set the pan over medium heat and bring the liquid to a simmer. Maintain a low simmer and stew the rhubarb until it is tender and starts falling apart, about 5 minutes. Transfer the rhubarb to a bowl and let cool slightly. The poached rhubarb can be stored in an airtight container in the refrigerator for up to 3 days.

4 To serve, divide the muesli among two bowls. Top with the poached rhubarb and toasted hazelnuts.

Grilled Peaches with Cashew Cream on Toast

This recipe is inspired by one of my favorite things in life: the combination of fruit, cheese, and honey. You can use whole-milk ricotta for this, but since I try to reduce my dairy intake, I have included a recipe for a savory cashew cream.

MAKES 4 SERVINGS

4 medium (1 pound or 454 g) ripe yet firm peaches, halved and pitted

2 teaspoons extra-virgin olive oil

½ cup Cashew Cream (recipe follows) or whole-milk ricotta

4 slices Sourdough Boules (page 103) or Nordic Rye-Style Seed Bread (page 101), toasted

2 tablespoons honey (preferably raw and local)

2 sprigs thyme

½ teaspoon freshly ground black pepper

1   Brush the cut sides of the peaches with the olive oil. Heat a cast-iron pan over medium-high heat. Place the peaches cut side down in the pan and cook until caramelized and slightly softened, about 3 minutes. Transfer the peaches onto a plate.

2   Spread the cashew cream over the toasted bread. Top with the peaches and a drizzle of honey. Pick the thyme leaves from the stems and let them fall on top of the peaches. Finish with pepper. Serve while the peaches are warm.

Cashew Cream

1½ cups (190 g) raw cashews

3 to 4 tablespoons filtered water, plus more for soaking

2 tablespoons freshly squeezed lemon juice

1 teaspoon kosher salt

I am usually not one for foods that are the fake version of something else, but this cashew cream stands strong on its own as a spread in open-faced sandwiches (pair with sliced tomato and a drizzle of olive oil) or as a dip to serve along with vegetables.

MAKES ABOUT 1 CUP

1   Put the cashews in a medium bowl, cover with cold water, and soak in the refrigerator overnight.

2   Drain the cashews and transfer them to a high-speed blender. Add the 3 tablespoons water, lemon juice, and salt. Process until smooth and creamy. Stop to scrape the sides with a spatula, then process again. You can add another tablespoon of water if the cream is too thick. Transfer to an airtight container and refrigerate for up to 1 week.

Cinnamon Buns

4 tablespoons (55 g) very soft
dairy-free butter, plus more
for greasing

2¼ cups (505 g) hemp milk
(page 21) or nut milk (page 20),
heated to 105 degrees F

2 tablespoons (50 g) honey

1 tablespoon (12 g) active dry
yeast

2 tablespoons (20 g) psyllium
husk powder

2 tablespoons (15 g) flaxseed
meal

1 cup (120 g) tapioca starch

¾ cup plus 1 tablespoon (120 g)
superfine brown rice flour,
plus more for dusting

¾ cup plus 1 tablespoon (120 g)
sorghum flour

4 teaspoons ground cinnamon,
divided

1½ teaspoons kosher salt

⅓ cup (70 g) granulated sugar

1 cup (120 g) powdered sugar

2 tablespoons hemp milk
(page 21) or almond milk
(page 20), at room temperature

1 teaspoon vanilla extract

This cinnamon bun recipe yields buns that are pillowy and soft. If dairy is not an issue for you, by all means use whole milk in place of the nut and hemp milks, and unsalted butter instead of the dairy-free kind. If you wanted to proof the dough overnight, you could retard the fermentation in the refrigerator and then bake it in the morning.

MAKES 8 SERVINGS

1   Grease the inside of a 10-inch cake pan with some butter. In a medium bowl, whisk together the heated hemp milk, honey, and yeast until dissolved. Let the mixture proof for 10 minutes, until foamy.

2   Whisk the psyllium powder and flaxseed meal into the yeast mixture, and let it gel for 5 minutes.

3   In the bowl of a stand mixer, whisk together the tapioca starch, brown rice flour, sorghum flour, 2 teaspoons of the cinnamon, and salt. Add the yeast gel and mix with the dough hook on medium speed for about 5 minutes, or until the dough comes together. The dough will be sticky.

4   Dust a work surface with some brown rice flour and scrape the dough onto it. Dust the top with more flour, and roll it to ⅛ to ¼ inch thick and about 15 by 13 inches.

5   In a bowl, mix together the butter, granulated sugar, and remaining 2 teaspoons cinnamon. Spread the mixture evenly on top of the dough. Roll the dough tightly into a log. Cut the log in half crosswise and then slice each half into four equal pieces. Place the buns in the greased cake pan, leaving space between. Cover the pan with plastic wrap and proof for 45 to 60 minutes, or until doubled.

6   Preheat the oven to 400 degrees F and bake the buns for about 50 minutes, until golden brown. Don't skimp on the time even if they look done on top as they take longer than normal cinnamon buns to really cook all the way through. Let them cool in the pan while you prepare the glaze.

7   In a medium bowl, whisk together the powdered sugar, hemp milk, and vanilla until smooth. Pour the glaze over the warm cinnamon buns and serve immediately.

Avocado, Smoked Salmon, and Cucumber on Toast

---

2 ripe medium avocados, halved and pitted

1 lime, zested and juiced

¼ teaspoon flaky sea salt, plus more for sprinkling

4 slices Nordic Rye-Style Seed Bread (page 101), toasted

8 ounces (225 g) smoked salmon (preferably wild), flaked into pieces

¼ medium cucumber, thinly sliced

1 small shallot or spring onion, thinly sliced

3 tablespoons chopped dill

3 tablespoons finely chopped chives

2 tablespoons extra-virgin olive oil

1 teaspoon freshly ground black pepper

You cannot go wrong with this combination of ingredients. It is a classic that is hard to improve, and as a part of my breakfast repertoire, it keeps me fueled and nourished for hours. I highly recommend making the Nordic Rye-Style Seed Bread that can be found on page 101. It is sour, crunchy, and deep in flavor, pairing beautifully with the sweet and creamy avocado and smoky salmon.

MAKES 4 SERVINGS

1 Scoop out pieces of avocado into a bowl using a spoon. You could mash it, but I prefer chunks of avocado on my toast. Toss it with the lime zest, juice, and salt.

2 Top the toasted bread with avocado, salmon, cucumber, shallot, dill, and chives. Drizzle with olive oil and sprinkle black pepper on top. You can also add a sprinkle of flaky salt if you are into it as much as I am. Serve immediately.

Rice Pudding with Plums

1¾ cups (395 g) water, divided
1 cup (200 g) arborio rice
½ teaspoon kosher salt
6 cups (1350 g) whole milk or almond milk (page 20)
⅓ cup (65 g) sugar
1 vanilla bean, split lengthwise and seeds scraped
1 orange
6 plums, halved and pitted
2 tablespoons coarsely chopped pistachios
2 tablespoons coconut flakes, toasted

This porridge-like breakfast is energizing while feeling like a special treat, even though it's not overly sweet. It can be served with any fruit, really; plums are just a favorite of mine. Orange juice–stewed dried fruit is great in the winter; use fresh berries in the summer.

MAKES 6 SERVINGS

1   Combine 1½ cups of the water, rice, and salt in a medium saucepan over medium heat. Cover and bring to a simmer, then reduce the heat to low and cook for 7 minutes, or until the water is almost completely absorbed. Stir in the milk, sugar, and vanilla bean and seeds. Using a vegetable peeler, peel a 3-inch piece of orange zest and add to the pan. Increase the heat to medium high and return to a simmer. Adjust the heat to maintain a gentle simmer and continue cooking, uncovered, stirring occasionally, for about 30 minutes, or until the rice is fully cooked and creamy.

2   Meanwhile, squeeze the juice of the orange into a small saucepan over high heat. Add the plums and remaining ¼ cup of water. Cook until the plums soften and create a light syrup, about 5 minutes. You can add a bit of sugar if the plums are too tart.

3   To serve, remove the vanilla bean and orange peel from the rice. Divide the rice among bowls and top with the plums, pistachios, and coconut.

Soft-Cooked Eggs with Dukkah and Bitter Greens on Toast

4 cold large eggs

6 cups chopped bitter greens, such as mustard greens, kale, or radicchio

½ teaspoon kosher salt

½ teaspoon freshly ground black pepper

3 tablespoons extra-virgin olive oil

2 teaspoons sunflower seed butter (page 28)

2 teaspoons apple cider vinegar

4 slices sourdough bread (page 103), toasted

4 tablespoons dukkah (page 40)

One of the most asked questions I receive is "How do you cook a perfect soft egg?" If you follow the instructions that follow, you should be able to achieve a perfectly soft-cooked egg every time—one where the white is cooked all the way through, the outer layer of the yolk is set, but the middle is still soft. The 7-minute time is for large eggs that are refrigerated. If your eggs are at room temperature or smaller than average, reduce the cooking time by 1½ minutes.

The dressing that is tossed with the bitter greens is one of the recipes my friends ask for constantly, and I always make extra to have on hand. Massage it into chopped kale and you will have a wonderful weeknight side salad.

MAKES 4 SERVINGS

1   Fill a medium pot halfway with water, or enough to cover the eggs. Bring the water to a boil over high heat. Gently lower the eggs into the boiling water, reduce the heat to medium low, cover the pot, and cook the eggs for 7 minutes. Make sure the water is simmering gently—a brisk boil could crack the eggs. Immediately remove the eggs from the pot and rinse them under cold water. When they are cool enough to handle, peel and set aside.

2   Wash the greens, and pat them dry with a towel. Toss them with the salt and pepper.

3   In a small bowl, whisk together the olive oil, sunflower butter, and vinegar. Pour the dressing over the greens and toss to coat evenly. I like to use clean hands for this as it allows me to really massage the dressing into the greens.

4   Pile the greens on top of the toasted sourdough. Cut each egg in half and place on top of the greens. The whites should be completely cooked and the yolks soft and slightly runny. Sprinkle 1 tablespoon dukkah on top of each egg and serve immediately.

Baked Eggs in Piperrada

¼ cup extra-virgin olive oil, plus more for drizzling

2 medium red onions, thinly sliced

1 green bell pepper, seeded and thinly sliced

1 red bell pepper, seeded and thinly sliced

1 teaspoon kosher salt

½ teaspoon freshly ground black pepper

½ teaspoon red pepper flakes

2 (14.5-ounce) cans whole peeled tomatoes (I like San Marzanos), drained

2 teaspoons sugar

8 large eggs

1 cup of tender greens, such as watercress, baby kale, or mustard greens

3 sprigs Italian parsley

3 sprigs dill

½ teaspoon piment d'Espelette (optional), see page 11 for description

Onions, peppers, and tomatoes are the Basque trifecta and a base for so many dishes. A *sofrito* of sorts. *Piperade* or *piperrada* (as we say in the Spanish side of the Basque Country) literally means "a whole load of peppers," and it is a dish my mom made often in the summer served alongside fried eggs or stewed meat. For this recipe, I add slightly more tomato than my mom would to create a sauce where the eggs can nestle and bake evenly. It is easy to make for a crowd. Be sure to serve it with thickly sliced bread to soak up all the sauce.

MAKES 4 TO 6 SERVINGS

1 Preheat the oven to 350 degrees F. Heat the oil in a large ovenproof skillet over medium heat. Add the onions, bell peppers, salt, black pepper, and red pepper flakes. Cook, stirring occasionally, until the vegetables are tender and caramelized, about 10 minutes.

2 Pour the tomatoes into a bowl, and squeeze them with clean hands to break them apart. Alternatively, you could puree them in a blender, but I like a bit more texture. Add the tomatoes to the skillet along with the sugar. Stir, taste, and adjust the seasoning—depending on how sweet the tomatoes are, you might need a bit more salt or pepper. Reduce the heat to medium low and cook the sauce for another 10 minutes.

3 Using a spoon, push the sauce to one side to make space for an egg. Crack the egg directly into the opening. The whites should be submerged in the sauce so they cook into it. Repeat with the remaining eggs.

4 Transfer the skillet to the oven and bake for 13 to 15 minutes, or until the egg whites are set and the yolks are soft. Top the eggs with the greens, parsley, dill, a sprinkle of piment d'Espelette, and a drizzle of olive oil. Serve while the eggs are hot.

Egg Tostada with Fennel, Radishes, and Yogurt

This is a fresh and light take on a breakfast tostada, which I make often for a midday snack. You can use corn or gluten-free flour tortillas, but make sure they are large enough so that an egg, once cracked, stays on. The egg gets a bit messy, but I love that—part of the yolk runny, part cooked. If you don't have fennel on hand, simply serve the tostada with avocado or any greens you have. It's also wonderful topped with sautéed mushrooms.

MAKES 4 SERVINGS

1 orange
1 teaspoon Dijon mustard
¼ teaspoon kosher salt
⅛ teaspoon freshly ground
  black pepper
5 teaspoons extra-virgin olive
  oil, divided
1 fennel bulb, thinly shaved
6 radishes, thinly shaved
¼ cup bitter greens or
  microgreens
2 sprigs dill
4 gluten-free flour or corn
  tortillas
4 large eggs
¼ cup (55 g) whole-milk yogurt
  (page 32)

1   Make the salad first. In a large bowl, zest the orange, then cut it in half and squeeze 2 teaspoons of juice. Whisk in the mustard, salt, and pepper, and then 3 teaspoons of the olive oil. Toss in the fennel, radishes, bitter greens, and dill. Set aside.

2   Heat a sauté pan over medium heat and add ½ teaspoon of the remaining olive oil. Place one tortilla at a time in the pan and cook until golden brown, about 30 seconds. Flip the tortilla and immediately crack an egg on top. The heat of the tortilla will begin to cook the egg white. Continue cooking for 1 minute. Flip the tortilla over one more time to finish cooking the egg, about 30 seconds. Slide onto a plate. Repeat with the remaining tortillas and eggs.

3   Top each hot tostada with 1 tablespoon of the yogurt and a quarter of the fennel salad. Serve immediately.

Sourdough Waffles with Carmelized Peaches

These waffles are incredible light, crispy, and tangy. Note that the starter must be fed and fermented overnight, so get started the evening before you plan to cook them. Not only are the waffles gluten-free, I also make them without dairy. However, if you prefer richer waffles, you can use homemade yogurt (page 32) in place of the coconut milk and melted unsalted butter instead of coconut oil. I serve these with caramelized peaches in the summer, but know that they can be topped with any fresh fruit or other caramelized fruits. I particularly love pears and apples.

MAKES 10 WAFFLES

For the sourdough waffles
1 cup (240 g) cold sourdough starter (page 59)
¾ cup (105 g) superfine brown rice flour
½ cup (60 g) tapioca starch
¾ cup (180 g) coconut milk (page 21) or almond milk (page 20)
¼ cup (55 g) freshly squeezed lemon juice
1 tablespoon honey (preferably raw and local)
1 large egg, lightly beaten
3 tablespoons melted coconut oil, plus more for greasing
2 teaspoons finely grated lemon zest
1 teaspoon vanilla extract
1 teaspoon baking soda
½ teaspoon kosher salt

For the caramelized peaches
2 tablespoons unsalted butter or coconut oil
1 vanilla bean, split lengthwise and seeds scraped
2 peaches, cut into wedges

1   The night before you are going to cook the waffles, whisk together the sourdough starter, brown rice flour, tapioca starch, coconut milk, lemon juice, and honey in a large bowl. Cover the bowl with plastic wrap and set aside for 8 to 12 hours at room temperature.

2   When you are ready to cook the waffles, preheat a waffle iron. Uncover the bowl with the starter mixture and add the egg, coconut oil, lemon zest, vanilla, baking soda, and salt to the bowl; whisk until combined. The batter will start bubbling up immediately.

3   Grease the waffle iron and pour in enough batter for one waffle, which will vary depending on the size of your iron. Cook until golden brown, 2 to 4 minutes. Repeat with remaining batter and serve hot.

4   While the waffles are cooking, heat a sauté pan over medium heat, and add the butter and vanilla bean and seeds. Swirl the butter around, then add the peaches. Cook for 1 to 2 minutes on each side, or until soft but not falling apart. Serve on top of the waffles.

Buckwheat Crêpes with Chocolate-Hazelnut Butter

2 cups (450 g) filtered water
1¼ cups (175 g) buckwheat flour
4 large eggs
¼ cup (55 g) extra-virgin olive oil
1 tablespoon sugar
½ teaspoon kosher salt
1 tablespoon melted unsalted
   butter or extra-virgin olive oil
½ cup Chocolate-Hazelnut
   Butter (page 29), at room
   temperature

Buckwheat crêpes are one of my favorite things to eat on weekend mornings. I like mine very thin, crispy, and lacy. A small amount of jam or nut butter is just enough to bring a balance of sweet and salty. You can also add caramelized peaches (page 91) or stewed plums (page 82) as a topping. Note that this batter is best after it has a chance to rest in the fridge overnight.

MAKES FIFTEEN 10-INCH CRÊPES

1 Combine the water, flour, eggs, olive oil, sugar, and salt in a blender, and puree on high speed until well mixed, about 30 seconds. You can use the batter right away, but I like to chill it in the refrigerator overnight, which allows the flour to hydrate fully and results in more flavor, elasticity, and crispness.

2 When you are ready to cook the crêpes, give the batter one good stir, especially if it has been resting in the refrigerator. Heat a nonstick crêpe pan over medium-high heat. Brush the pan with a little bit of the melted butter, then pour in about ⅓ cup of the batter while swirling the pan to ensure it goes in as a thin layer. Small bubbles will appear around the batter as it cooks. Tuck in the edges with a rubber spatula and cook for 30 seconds, or until golden. Grab an edge with your fingers and gently flip the crêpe over, or use a spatula if the pan is too hot. Finish cooking for another 30 seconds, then slide onto a plate. Repeat with the remaining batter.

3 Spread about 1 teaspoon of the Chocolate-Hazelnut Butter over half of each crêpe, fold, and serve immediately while warm. Any leftover batter can be stored in an airtight container in the refrigerator for up to 3 days.

Raspberry Pancakes with Maple Yogurt

½ cup (115 g) whole-milk yogurt
  (page 32)
3 tablespoons maple syrup,
  divided
⅔ cup (75 g) gluten-free oat flour
⅔ cup (65 g) almond flour
¼ cup (30 g) tapioca starch
1 tablespoon baking powder
½ teaspoon kosher salt
½ cup (115 g) whole milk or
  almond milk (page 20)
2 large eggs, separated
1 tablespoon vanilla extract
1 cup (125 g) raspberries,
  mashed once with a fork
2 tablespoons unsalted butter

There is always the debate in my house about fruit as a pancake topping, which is my children's favorite, versus folding the fruit into the batter and cooking it, which is my preference. In this case, I opted for sharing how I like my pancakes—extra moist from the incorporated juices of the fruit. You can, of course, simply leave the raspberries out of the batter and use them as a topping.

The trick for this pancake recipe is to separate the egg whites individually and incorporate more air into the batter. The result is very light and fluffy pancakes. The almond and oat flours give the pancakes texture and a warm nutty flavor.

MAKES 10 PANCAKES

1 Whisk together the yogurt with 1 tablespoon of the maple syrup. Set aside.

2 In a medium bowl, whisk together the flours, tapioca starch, baking powder, and salt. Whisk in the milk, remaining 2 tablespoons maple syrup, egg yolks, and vanilla. Let the batter sit for 5 minutes.

3 Meanwhile, in a clean bowl, whip the egg whites to soft peaks. Fold them into the batter, being careful not to deflate it too much, then fold in the raspberries to create a ripple.

4 Heat a griddle or cast-iron pan over medium heat. Add a dab of butter to the pan and pour in ⅓ cup of the batter. You can cook multiple pancakes at a time if you have a large enough pan. Cook until bubbles appear on the surface, about 3 minutes, then flip the pancakes over and continue cooking for another 2 or 3 minutes until set. Repeat with the remaining batter, adding a dab of butter to the pan every time. Any unused batter can be refrigerated for 1 day. Serve the pancakes with the maple yogurt.

CHAPTER THREE

Baking

Our days are too often passed in a rapid flurry of checklists and traffic and emails. The importance of slowing down is by no means new, but I believe that each of us should find a practice that leaves us feeling both quiet and fulfilled. For some, that's a moment of meditation. For others, a trip to the gym. I quell that constant buzzing by working with my hands, occupying my body as I occupy my mind, distracting it from the stresses of the day. Baking is my go-to when I want to allow some space. Kneading sourdough bread, rolling pastry dough, whisking cake batter: these mindless activities pull me in through their repetition, making me trancelike in the process. The simplicity lulls the noise of the mind while the exactness of measurement requires clear focus. It's the perfect balance between right and left brain, the romance of creativity and the exactitude of science.

A number of these recipes are rather quick, such as the One-Bowl Apricot and Olive Oil Cake (page 128) or the Banana Bread with Sunflower Seed Icing (page 136), but others can be a bit more time-consuming, such as the Gâteau Basque (page 124) and both of the sourdough breads. I encourage you to take the time to let baking serve as a meditative activity.

See page 6 for how to substitute gluten-free flours.

Nordic Rye-Style Seed Bread

1 cup (140 g) raw sunflower seeds
½ cup (90 g) raw buckwheat
  groats
4 cups (900 g) filtered water,
  divided
¾ cup (200 g) cold sourdough
  starter (page 59)
⅔ cup (90 g) superfine brown
  rice flour, plus more for dusting
3 tablespoons (30 g) psyllium
  husk powder
1 cup (140 g) sorghum flour
1 cup (140 g) buckwheat flour
¼ cup (30 g) tapioca starch
2 tablespoons molasses
2 teaspoons kosher salt
Extra-virgin olive oil, for greasing

Note: For a variation on this
recipe, you can replace the
sunflower seeds with pumpkin
seeds and add 1 tablespoon of
caraway seeds to the dough.

I grew up with crusty baguettes and rich brioches. Dark, dense breads were not on my radar until I traveled to Germany for the first time as a teenager. I was backpacking through small towns with little money to spend in restaurants, and consequently, my meals consisted mainly of sandwiches I prepared with bread from local bakeries and charcuterie from the butcher shops. That's when I discovered rich, dense, dark, sour rye breads. I returned to the Basque Country after that trip, seeking out specialty shops that sold imported, packaged dark-rye breads. While what I found was not what I had tasted back in Germany, it did the trick and solidified my devotion to Nordic-style breads.

My version is dark and sour with buckwheat and molasses. The buckwheat groats and sunflower seeds add a nice crunchy texture. I mill my own buckwheat flour with raw buckwheat groats that I grind in a high-speed blender. You can also use dark buckwheat flour for a more intense flavor. Don't expect this loaf to yield a light crumb. It is certainly moist but also quite dense. It's perfect thinly sliced for morning toast or open-faced sandwiches.

MAKES 1 LOAF

1   In a medium bowl, combine the sunflower seeds, buckwheat groats, and 2 cups (450 g) of the water. Cover the bowl with plastic wrap and set aside at room temperature for 8 hours or overnight.

2   In another medium bowl, whisk together the sourdough starter, brown rice flour, and ½ cup (112 g) of the water. Cover the bowl with plastic wrap and set aside at room temperature for 8 hours or overnight.

3   In the morning, whisk together the psyllium powder and remaining 1½ cups (336 g) water until it gels.

4   Drain the sunflower seeds and buckwheat groats in a colander and transfer to the bowl of a stand mixer. Add the sorghum and buckwheat flours, tapioca starch, molasses, salt, sourdough starter, and psyllium gel. Mix with the dough hook on medium speed until the dough comes together, about 2 minutes. It will be wet and sticky, much like thick cake batter. $\longrightarrow$

5   Brush the inside of a 1-pound loaf pan with olive oil and dust with brown rice flour. Shake off any excess flour. Spoon the dough into the loaf pan and even out the top with a spatula or wet hands. Cover the pan loosely with plastic wrap and set aside at room temperature (ideally around 70 degrees F) for 3 to 4 hours. If your kitchen is too cold, place the pan in the oven with the oven light on. In the summer you can set the dough on the counter and reduce fermentation time to 2 hours.

6   Preheat the oven to 450 degrees F and set a rack in the middle. Remove the plastic wrap and dust the dough with brown rice flour. Using the tip of a sharp knife, score the top of the dough lengthwise. Bake for 30 minutes, then reduce the heat to 400 degrees F and bake for an additional 45 minutes. Carefully turn the bread out of the pan, and place it directly on the oven rack. Bake for an additional 20 to 30 minutes, depending how dark you like your crust (I like mine very caramelized).

7   Transfer the bread to a cooling rack, and let it cool completely before cutting. Store the bread wrapped in parchment or plastic wrap at room temperature. It is best eaten within 3 days. You can also freeze the bread once completely cooled for up to 3 months.

Sourdough Boules

For the starter

1 cup (280 g) cold sourdough
    starter (page 59)
1 cup plus 2 tablespoons (160 g)
    superfine brown rice flour,
    plus more for dusting
1 cup (225 g) filtered water, at
    room temperature

For the dough

1¾ cups (210 g) gluten-free oat
    flour, plus more for dusting
1 cup (120 g) tapioca starch
¾ cup (120 g) potato starch
1 cup *minus* 1 tablespoon (120 g)
    sorghum flour
2 teaspoons kosher salt
¼ cup (40 g) psyllium husk
    powder
¼ cup (25 g) flaxseed meal
3 cups plus 2 tablespoons
    (700 g) filtered water, at
    room temperature

I have been making this bread nearly every other day since 2016. It's fairly simple, and I now know every measurement by heart. It requires only time and a healthy sourdough starter (see page 59 to make your own). I make two boules at a time because that's how much my oven can handle, but seriously, if I had more space, I'd bake two or three times as many because my friends go crazy for it.

The bread has a very moist interior with a tender crumb and a crusty exterior that is quite addicting. Many people I serve this bread to are surprised to learn that it's gluten-free. It's that good! The beautiful shape is obtained by proofing the bread in *bannetons*, or wicker proofing baskets, which you can find for around twenty dollars at most cooking stores and online.

MAKES 2 BOULES

1 Prepare the starter the night before you are going to bake the bread. In a large bowl, stir together the sourdough starter, brown rice flour, and water. Cover the bowl with plastic wrap and set aside at room temperature for 8 to 10 hours, or overnight, until bubbly. There may be some separation, with the top being thick and the bottom more liquid—this is normal.

2 In the morning, prepare the dough. In the bowl of a stand mixer, whisk together the oat flour, tapioca starch, potato starch, sorghum flour, and salt.

3 In a large bowl, whisk together the psyllium powder, flaxseed meal, and water. This mixture will quickly become thick and gel-like. Add this to the dry ingredients along with the sourdough starter. Mix with the dough hook on medium speed until the dough comes together and all the flour has been incorporated, about 3 minutes.

4 Transfer the dough to a lightly floured surface, and cut it into two equal pieces (each one should be about 2 pounds, or 1 kg). Knead each half lightly, shaping it into a ball. The dough should be moist and hold its shape.

5 Dust two proofing baskets or mixing bowls with superfine brown rice flour. Gently transfer the dough rounds into the baskets with the dough seam facing up. Cover the baskets $\longrightarrow$

loosely with plastic wrap and place in a warm spot (ideally between 70 and 75 degrees F)—I usually put mine in the oven with the oven light on. Proof the dough for 3 hours. In the summer you can set the dough on the counter and reduce fermentation time to 2 hours. The dough is ready to bake when it feels springy and soft.

6 Approximately 30 minutes before baking, preheat the oven to 500 degrees F and place two cast-iron Dutch ovens inside for at least 20 minutes on the lower rack of the oven. When the dough is ready, invert each basket onto your clean hand and gently place one round into each pot. Score the top two or three times, dust with a bit of oat flour, and add a couple of ice cubes to the side of the dough in each pot. Cover the Dutch ovens with their lids and bake the dough for 45 minutes. Uncover, reduce the heat to 450 degrees F, and bake for an additional 50 minutes, until the crusts are dark and the bread sounds hollow when tapped.

7 Transfer the boules onto a cooling rack, and let them cool *completely* before cutting. This is very important because cooling allows the crumb to set; if you cut it too soon, the bread will collapse and become gummy. Be patient. Store the bread in a brown paper bag at room temperature. It is best eaten within 2 days. You can also freeze the bread once completely cooled for up to 3 months.

Gluten-Free Bread Baking Tips

Conquering the task of creating gluten-free breads feels like the pinnacle of my accomplishments. I have tested and retested recipes ever since I was diagnosed with gluten intolerance in 2010, but the bounce and texture that comes from gluten was tricky to replicate without the protein. It's always a work in progress as new ingredients surface in the market, and I continue to learn new science and technique. I have stopped using any xanthan gum in my breads and rely on psyllium husk powder as the main binder, which is substantially easier to digest and results in much better crumb texture. Gluten-free breads need a lot of moisture, and psyllium can absorb large amounts of it, creating a gel that provides both hold and elasticity. This also means that my yeast breads rarely rely on eggs, making them suitable for anyone adhering to a vegan diet or those with an egg intolerance.

I want to reiterate the importance of weighing ingredients here. I have provided volume measurements for all recipes for your convenience, but I would highly recommend you use a scale, even when measuring liquids. It will help you with consistency and perfect texture every time. Digital kitchen scales are inexpensive and widely available. I couldn't bake without mine.

You will notice my gluten-free bread recipes bake for a long time, some nearly 90 minutes. That is because the recipes are high in moisture—you must give that moisture time to evaporate and for the crumb to set. So even if your bread looks baked on the outside, it will need all that time to set on the inside.

Be sure not to overproof the dough—if overproofed, the crumb will detach from the crust, become gummy, and won't fully bake through.

My final important tip is to let yeast breads cool completely after baking. I mean it. It's crucial to set the crumb with all its airiness. Again, these loaves are high in moisture. If any tinge of steam is left in the loaf, the crumb collapses a bit onto itself and it will become gummy. Once the loaf is completely cool and dry, a serrated knife will cut easily and you will notice the air pockets throughout the crumb. Then you can really enjoy your masterpiece.

Buckwheat Sweet Yeast Bread with Dried Apricots and Walnuts

I love baking this scented and sweet yeast bread in the winter and serving it with thick cultured butter and cheese. You can substitute the walnuts for other nuts, and the apricots can be substituted with other dried fruits such as cherries, cranberries, raisins, or figs. When the loaf has dried out after a couple of days, I love to slice it very thinly and bake it in the oven at 300 degrees F—almost as if you were making biscotti—to create crackers that can be served on a cheese plate.

MAKES 1 BOULE

2¼ cups (505 g) whole milk or almond milk (page 20), heated to 110 degrees F

3 tablespoons (75 g) dark unsulphured molasses

1 tablespoon (12 g) active dry yeast

3 tablespoons (30 g) psyllium husk powder

2 cups (240 g) buckwheat flour, plus more for dusting

1 cup (120 g) tapioca starch

2 teaspoons finely grated orange zest

2 teaspoons finely grated lemon zest

2 teaspoons finely grated peeled ginger

2 teaspoons ground cinnamon

1½ teaspoons kosher salt

1 cup (100 g) coarsely chopped dried apricots

½ cup (50 g) coarsely chopped walnuts

1   In a large bowl, whisk together the warm milk, molasses, and yeast until dissolved. Let the yeast activate for about 10 minutes, or until frothy. Whisk in the psyllium powder and allow the mixture to gel for 5 minutes.

2   In the bowl of a stand mixer, combine the buckwheat flour, tapioca starch, orange and lemon zests, ginger, cinnamon, and salt. Add the yeast mixture and mix with the dough hook on medium speed until the dough comes together, about 2 minutes. Add the apricots and walnuts and continue mixing for 1 minute. The dough will feel very sticky, but it will come together with a little bit of flour.

3   Dust a work surface with the buckwheat flour. Scrape out the dough and shape it into a ball, dusting with more flour if needed. Dust a proofing basket or mixing bowl with buckwheat flour, and place the dough in it. Cover with plastic wrap and set aside to proof at room temperature for 45 to 60 minutes.

4   While the dough is proofing, place a cast-iron Dutch oven in the oven and preheat to 450 degrees F. When the dough is ready, turn it out onto your clean hand and gently place it inside the heated Dutch oven. Cover with the lid and bake for 30 minutes. Uncover, reduce the heat to 400 degrees F, and continue baking for another 30 minutes, until golden brown. The crust will be thin and crispy and the interior moist. Transfer the dough to a cooling rack and cool completely before cutting, at least 1 hour. It's very important to let all the steam evaporate and the crumb set before cutting. Store the bread at room temperature wrapped in parchment or a brown paper bag for up to 3 days.

Black Olive, Caraway, and Honey Yeast Bread

The words *yeast* and *honey* immediately evoke a sense of comfort in me. They remind me of the honey buns of my youth that I would eat straight out of the oven with a slice of Idiazábal cheese. Sweet and tender bread with something briny and salty. A loaf of this bread with black olives is a staple in my house these days. It makes the perfect sandwich bread with a thin crust and tender crumb. You can easily omit the olives and caraway to have a plain but equally satisfying loaf.

MAKES 1 LOAF

1 teaspoon extra-virgin olive oil, for greasing
¾ cup (105 g) superfine brown rice flour, plus more for dusting
1 tablespoon (25 g) honey
2 teaspoons (8 g) active dry yeast
1⅔ cups (400 g) filtered water, heated to 110 degrees F
4 teaspoons (15 g) psyllium husk powder
¾ cup (105 g) sorghum flour
¾ cup (90 g) tapioca starch
1 tablespoon caraway seeds
1½ teaspoons kosher salt
¾ cup (90 g) pitted black olives, roughly chopped
1 tablespoon apple cider vinegar

1 Brush the bottom and sides of a 9-by-4-inch loaf pan with the olive oil. Dust the inside with brown rice flour.

2 In a medium bowl, whisk together the honey, yeast, and water. Set aside to proof for 10 minutes. Whisk in the psyllium powder, and let it gel for 5 to 10 minutes.

3 In the bowl of a stand mixer, whisk together the brown rice flour, sorghum flour, tapioca starch, caraway seeds, and salt. Add the black olives, apple cider vinegar, and yeast mixture to the bowl. Mix with the dough hook on medium speed until it comes together into a moist and loose dough, about 2 minutes.

4 Dust a work surface with brown rice flour, and turn the dough out onto it. Knead the dough a couple of times, shaping it into a loose log about 9 inches long. Gently transfer the dough to the loaf pan. Cover with a clean linen towel or plastic wrap and set aside to proof at room temperature for 1 hour, or until doubled.

5 Preheat the oven to 425 degrees F. Dust the top of the dough with brown rice flour. Bake the bread for 1 hour. Carefully turn the bread out of the pan, and place it directly on the oven rack. Bake for an additional 45 minutes.

6 Transfer the bread to a cooling rack and cool completely before cutting. The bread needs to set in the center as the steam evaporates otherwise it will have a gummy crumb. I often bake it at night and wait until the morning to eat it. This bread keeps best wrapped in a clean kitchen towel or parchment paper for up to 3 days.

Plum Frangipane Tart

Superfine brown rice flour,
   for dusting
½ recipe 3-2-1 Pie Dough
   (recipe follows)
1 cup (100 g) hazelnut or
   almond flour
½ cup (100 g) granulated sugar
7 tablespoons (100 g) very soft
   (not melted) unsalted butter
1 large egg
1 tablespoon dark rum (optional)
½ teaspoon kosher salt
6 to 8 plums, halved and pitted
¼ cup hazelnuts, toasted and
   coarsely chopped (optional)
¼ cup white currants (optional)
Powdered sugar, for dusting

Note: The frangipane filling
freezes well, and this recipe
can easily be doubled. You can
store the filling in the freezer for
up to 3 months. Thaw it in the
refrigerator for 24 hours before
assembling the tart.

The filling of this tart is what is known in pastry as frangipane cream. It is my go-to filling for fruit tarts because it is creamy and luxuriously rich. It is also a really simple recipe to remember: 100 grams nut flour, 100 grams sugar, 100 grams butter, 1 egg, pinch of salt. It's so easy to have this gorgeous, fresh dessert practically on hand: keep some frozen pie dough in the freezer (see page 114), pick fruit from a tree, refer to this recipe, and you will have the most decadent yet simple tart you can imagine. I call for plums here, but it also works great with peaches, nectarines, apricots, pears, apples, quince, cherries, or berries.

MAKES ONE 9-INCH TART

1 Preheat the oven to 400 degrees F.

2 Dust a work surface with brown rice flour. Roll out the pie dough to ⅛ inch thick, then transfer it into a tart pan. If the dough cracks, which happens if it is too cold, pinch it back together. Gently press the dough into the pan, trimming off any excess, and place in the refrigerator to chill while you prepare the filling.

3 In a bowl, stir together the hazelnut flour, granulated sugar, butter, egg, rum, and salt with a wooden spoon until creamy. Alternatively, you could blend the filling in a food processor. Make sure the butter is well incorporated with no large pieces, otherwise it will ooze out of the tart while baking.

4 Spread the filling evenly over the chilled tart dough. Top with the plums, cut sides up, so they're tucked tightly against each other and pressed slightly into the frangipane.

5 Place the tart pan on a baking sheet and bake until golden brown and set, 45 to 50 minutes. Let the tart cool for 15 minutes before unmolding.

6 Scatter the hazelnuts and white currants over the tart. Dust with powdered sugar and serve.

Pie Dough 3-2-1

1½ cups (210 g) superfine
  brown rice flour, plus
  more for dusting
½ cup (80 g) potato starch
½ cup (60 g) tapioca starch
½ teaspoon kosher salt
1 cup (225 g) cold unsalted
  butter, cut into ½-inch
  dice
6 to 7 tablespoons (110 g)
  ice-cold water

When I was a pastry student at the Florida Culinary Institute, my instructor Chef Schmidtke drilled the importance of ratios into our head. "Always remember these ratios. They will serve you any time you need to make a tart or buttercream for a cake in a pinch!" he said repeatedly. He was right. Those basic recipes for pie dough, pastry cream, buttercream, and more are the building blocks to many of my recipes today.

This 3-2-1 pie dough is 3 parts flour, 2 parts cold butter, and 1 part ice water, plus a pinch of salt. All the ratios are calculated by weight measures, of course. If you add up the amounts by volume, it is not strictly 3-2-1, but it is close enough.

You can blend your own gluten-free flours to make different flavor profiles as well. Buckwheat adds earthiness, sorghum is slightly sweeter and closer to wheat flavor, and nut flours provide texture and crumb to make starchier doughs that have a bit more flake. As a guideline, I usually like to have about 60 percent whole-grain and 40 percent starch, but play around and see how you can enhance a filling by adjusting the crust flavors and textures.

What follows is a double-crust recipe, but you can make as much dough as you need, keeping the 3-2-1 ratio in mind. Another helpful bit of knowledge: you need about 1 ounce of dough per inch of tart, so if you are making a pie that is about 9 inches, you should use about 9 ounces of dough. This is an estimate that has always helped me when working with different tart pans and pie dishes.

MAKES ENOUGH FOR TWO 9-INCH TARTS

1 Combine the brown rice flour, potato starch, tapioca starch, and salt in the bowl of a food processor. Pulse a few times to aerate the flour. Add the diced butter and pulse about ten times, or until the butter is the size of peas. Alternatively, you could do this by hand, working the butter into the flour with

clean fingertips. Add 6 tablespoons ice water and pulse until the dough starts coming together. Check the dough by pressing it between your fingers. Depending on humidity, you might not need all the ice water, which is why I start with less. Add the remaining tablespoon if the dough seems too dry and crumbly—it should stick together without feeling wet.

2   Transfer the dough onto a work surface, and bring it together without handling it too much. The warmth of your hands can melt the butter, and we want to keep it cold. Cold butter aids in creating a flaky crust.

3   Cut the dough into two equal pieces. Wrap them in parchment paper and flatten slightly. Chill the dough in the refrigerator for at least 30 minutes. You can also freeze the dough at this point, which I do often. Wrap it in plastic wrap and freeze for up to 3 months. Then thaw it out in the refrigerator when you are ready to use it.

4   To roll the dough, dust a work surface with brown rice flour. Start rolling the dough from the center outward, turning it 90 degrees every time. Make sure the surface and rolling pin are well floured to avoid sticking. Sometimes, especially if it's too cold, the dough will tend to crack. If this happens, bring the dough back together and knead it a couple of times to give it elasticity and warm it slightly.

Caramelized Apple Galette

4 (1½ pounds or 680 g) firm
    and juicy apples, such as
    Honeycrisp
½ cup (100 g) sugar, plus more
    for sprinkling
2 tablespoons unsalted butter
2 tablespoons apple cider vinegar
1 tablespoon ground cinnamon
1 tablespoon vanilla extract
Tapioca starch, for dusting
½ recipe Puff Pastry
    with Cultured Butter
    (recipe follows), unbaked
½ cup (50 g) almond flour
1 large egg, lightly beaten

This galette is a reversed version of a classic apple tarte tatin, as the caramel-cooked apples are encased in puff pastry rather than being arranged on top. This galette has more crust, which is always my preference. You could also make this galette with caramelized quince or pear.

MAKES ONE 9-INCH GALETTE

1   Preheat the oven to 425 degrees F, and line a baking sheet with parchment paper. Peel, core, and quarter the apples.

2   Heat a large stainless steel sauté pan over medium-high heat. Sprinkle the sugar evenly around the pan and cook until it turns a deep caramel color. If the sugar is not melting evenly, stir it with a wooden spoon to incorporate any coarse areas into the melting ones. Once the sugar has turned into caramel, carefully stir in the butter, vinegar, cinnamon, and vanilla with a wooden spoon. The hot sugar may bubble up, so stand away from the pan if necessary. Add the apples and reduce the heat to low. Swirl the pan so the apples are evenly distributed and in a single layer. Cook the apples for 7 minutes, or until tender. Remove the pan from the heat, and let the apples cool for a few minutes until lukewarm and cool enough to handle.

3   Dust a work surface with the tapioca starch. Roll the puff pastry dough into an imperfect circle about 12 inches in diameter. Transfer the dough to the baking sheet. Sprinkle the almond flour in the center of the dough, then pile the apples on top, leaving a 3-inch border around. There may be some caramel left in the pan, which can be saved to drizzle over the galette after baking. Fold the pastry edges over the filling. If the dough is getting too warm, place in the refrigerator for 15 minutes to make sure it's nice and cold before baking.

4   Brush the dough with the egg, and sprinkle sugar all over the top. Bake for 35 to 40 minutes, until the crust is golden brown. Wait a few minutes before cutting the galette so it has a chance to settle and doesn't crumble.

STEP 1

STEP 2

STEP 3

STEP 4

Puff Pastry with Cultured Butter

¾ cup (90 g) tapioca starch, plus more for dusting

⅔ cup (110 g) potato starch

½ cup (70 g) sweet white rice flour

½ cup (70 g) superfine brown rice flour, plus 1 heaping tablespoon for the butter packet

½ cup (70 g) sorghum flour

1¼ teaspoons xanthan gum

1 teaspoon sea salt

1½ cups (345 g) cold unsalted cultured butter (page 24), divided

¾ cup plus 2 tablespoons (185 g) ice-cold water, plus more as needed

The smell of flour and copious amounts of butter baking in the oven together immediately transports me to my childhood. It is as if my lips can still taste the *palmiers* and mille-feuilles my grandfather was known for.

Puff pastry takes time. You will need a couple hours because you must be very diligent about chilling the dough between turns—this is how to achieve perfect layers. The steam that butter creates during baking lifts up the thin layers of dough, giving it crunch and flakiness. Because this recipe does not contain gluten, the dough isn't as elastic as traditional recipes made with wheat flour. Be gentle with it. If the dough cracks, gently pinch it back together, but again, be mindful of shaping it right and keeping the butter layered. It is also temperature sensitive, so in summer months you will have to work a bit quicker than in the winter.

MAKES 2 POUNDS PUFF PASTRY

1   In a large bowl, whisk together the tapioca starch, potato starch, rice flours, sorghum flour, xanthan gum, and salt. Cut ½ cup (115 g) of the butter into ½-inch pieces and add to the flour mixture. Work the butter into the flour with clean fingertips until it resembles coarse, loose sand. Add the ice water and mix with a wooden spoon until the dough comes together. It may seem a bit dry and stiff at this point, but the dough will come together when kneading. You can add another teaspoon of ice water if it does seem too dry.

2   Transfer the dough to a work surface, and knead it into a ball. Continue kneading until the dough is smooth and free of cracks, about 7 minutes. If the dough keeps cracking, wet your fingers and let the dough absorb that bit of moisture, but don't add too much water at once. Shape the dough into a 5-inch square about 2 inches thick. Wrap the dough in plastic and refrigerate while you prepare the butter packet.

3   Clean off the work surface, and lay out a sheet of plastic wrap. Place the remaining 1 cup (230 g) butter in the center of the plastic wrap. Dust the top of the butter with the heaping tablespoon brown rice flour. Cover the butter with another sheet of plastic wrap. Using a rolling pin, pound the butter ⟶

flat into a rectangle. Remove the top plastic layer, and fold the butter onto itself. Gather any leftover brown rice flour, and sprinkle it across top. Cover the butter with the plastic wrap once again, then flatten it again. Repeat this process five times until you have a butter square that is about 5 inches square and ½ inch tall. If it's warm in your kitchen, wrap the butter in plastic and refrigerate for 10 to 15 minutes.

4   Dust the work surface with a little tapioca starch to prevent sticking. Place the chilled dough on top and, starting in the center, roll out the four sides of the dough to form a square with four flaps. The center of the dough should be about the size of the butter packet, and the flaps should be long enough that you can fold them over the butter completely. The flap ends tend to be rounded, so gently square them off with your hands so they fit the squared edges of the butter packet nicely. Set the butter packet in the center of the dough, and fold all four flaps over the butter. Pinch closed any cracks—none of the butter should be exposed.

5   Using a rolling pin, roll out the dough with butter packet to form a rectangle that's approximately 6 inches by 18 inches. The exact size doesn't matter, but you want the rectangle to be about three times as long as it is wide. Fold one-third of the dough over the middle third, and then fold the other third over that (this is called a letter fold). Rotate the dough 90 degrees. Roll the dough out again until it's three times as long as it is wide, and fold one-third over the middle third and then the other third over that. This is the second letter fold. Make sure you are pinching any cracks together as you go. Using a pastry brush, dust off any excess tapioca starch from the dough. The cleaner and neater you work at every step, the better the puff will be in the oven. Wrap the dough with plastic wrap and refrigerate for 1 hour.

6 Remove the dough from the fridge, and let it rest at room temperature for 10 to 15 minutes. The dough needs to be pliable but cold. If the dough is too cold and hard, it will crack, but if the butter gets too soft, it will tend to ooze out. Dust a work surface and the top of the dough with tapioca starch. Once again, roll the dough into a rectangle that's three times as long as it is wide. Do a third letter fold. Rotate 90 degrees, roll again, and fold as indicated for the fourth time. Dust off any excess tapioca starch. Wrap the dough in plastic wrap and chill for another hour.

7 Remove the dough from the fridge, and let it rest at room temperature for 10 to 15 minutes. Repeat the rolling and folding process twice more, turning the dough 90 degrees after each one. You will have six letter folds by this time. Wrap the dough in plastic wrap and chill in the fridge for a final hour.

8 After this, the dough is ready to be used in your favorite recipes. It will keep in the refrigerator for up to 2 days. If you are not going to use it right away, cut the dough in half, and roll it into ¼-inch-thick sheets. Place the puff pastry sheets on a baking sheet lined with parchment paper with parchment between each pastry sheet. Wrap the baking sheet with plastic wrap and freeze. The dough can be stored this way in the freezer for 3 months. To thaw, transfer the pastry to the refrigerator for a few hours. Do not thaw at room temperature.

Fig, Taleggio, and Pine Nut Tart

This is one of those hearty, savory tarts that are perfect in late summer or early fall when figs are at their best. But don't fret: you can make this tart all year-round even when they're not in season. I love it with pears and apples. Taleggio is a soft, ripened Italian cheese that melts really well. If you cannot find Taleggio, you could use fontina or *robiola*.

MAKES ONE 9-INCH TART

Superfine brown rice flour,
    for dusting
½ recipe pie dough (page 114), or
    1 sheet puff pastry (page 119)
2 tablespoons extra-virgin
    olive oil
1 small leek (white part only),
    halved lengthwise and sliced
    (about ½ cup)
1 clove garlic, minced
3 tablespoons finely chopped
    tender herbs (parsley,
    tarragon, dill, chives)
3 ounces (85 g) Taleggio, sliced
½ cup (115 g) crème fraîche
    (page 26) or heavy cream
1 large egg
½ teaspoon kosher salt
6 ripe figs, halved
2 tablespoons raw pine nuts

1   Preheat the oven to 375 degrees F.

2   Dust a work surface with brown rice flour. Roll out the dough to ⅛ inch thick, then transfer it into a tart pan. Gently press the dough into the pan, trim off any excess, and place in the freezer for 10 minutes.

3   Place the tart pan on a baking sheet (in case any butter oozes out while baking). Cover the tart with parchment paper and top with pie weights or dry beans. Bake the tart for 20 minutes, remove the weights and parchment, then bake for an additional 5 minutes, until golden.

4   Meanwhile, make the filling. Heat the olive oil in a medium sauté pan over medium heat. Add the leeks and garlic and cook, stirring occasionally, until soft, about 3 minutes. Stir in the herbs, then spread the mixture inside the tart crust. Top with the Taleggio slices.

5   In a small bowl, whisk together the crème fraîche, egg, and salt, then pour this over the leek filling. Nestle in the fig halves, cut side up, and sprinkle with the pine nuts.

6   Return the tart pan to the baking sheet and bake for 30 to 35 minutes, until golden brown. Let the tart cool in the pan for 10 minutes before unmolding. Serve warm or at room temperature.

Gâteau Basque

For the custard
1½ cups (340 g) whole milk
½ cup (100 g) light brown sugar, divided
1 vanilla bean, split lengthwise and seeds scraped
1 medium lemon
3 egg yolks
¼ cup (55 g) heavy cream
¼ cup (30 g) cornstarch

For the pastry
1 cup (225 g) very soft unsalted butter, plus more for greasing
1 cup (200 g) light brown sugar
1 vanilla bean, split lengthwise and seeds scraped
4 whole eggs, at room temperature
1 cup (140 g) superfine brown rice flour
1 cup (160 g) potato starch
1¼ cups (125 g) almond flour
1 teaspoon baking powder
1 teaspoon kosher salt

The Basque Country is divided between Spain and France. The North in France (*iparralde*, as we call it) speaks Basque with a French accent, and the South in Spain (*hegoalde*) speaks Basque—well, you guessed it—with a Spanish accent. Until the European Union eliminated all borders, we had to bring our passports anytime we traveled to the North. There was always tension felt at the border and exhilaration once we made it through. I loved driving those sixty miles to simply eat some Gâteau Basque at centuries-old Maison Adam. The pastry was very popular in the North and hard to find in the South, its buttery crust filled with creamy custard or preserves from nearby jam makers. The pastry is somewhere between a tart and a cake, and oftentimes, the top is decorated with a *lauburu*, the symbol of Basque unity.

MAKES ONE 9-INCH TART

1   First, make the custard. Combine the milk, ¼ cup of the brown sugar, and the vanilla bean and seeds in a medium saucepan. Using a vegetable peeler, cut three strips of lemon rind (avoiding the white pith) and add it to the milk. Bring the milk to a simmer, turn the heat off, and steep the milk for 5 minutes.

2   In a large bowl, whisk together the egg yolks, remaining ¼ cup brown sugar, heavy cream, and cornstarch together until smooth. Return the milk to a simmer, and pour it over the egg mixture while whisking constantly. Strain this custard base through a fine-mesh sieve back into the saucepan. Cook over medium heat, whisking constantly. As soon as the custard thickens, about 2 minutes, transfer the custard into a clean bowl. Cover the surface of the custard with plastic wrap, making sure the plastic is pressed against it, which will help keep the custard from developing a thin skin on top. Let the custard cool completely before proceeding. You can make it 1 day in advance and keep it in the refrigerator.

3   Next, make the pastry. In the bowl of a stand mixer, combine the butter, brown sugar, and vanilla seeds. Using the paddle attachment, mix on medium-high speed until very creamy, about 3 minutes. Scrape the sides of the bowl and the paddle to make sure everything is really well mixed.

4   Add 3 of the eggs, one at a time, while the mixer is running, waiting to add the next one until each is well incorporated. Scrape the sides of the bowl and the paddle once again.

5   In a small bowl, whisk together the brown rice flour, potato starch, almond flour, baking powder, and salt. Add the dry ingredients to the mixing bowl. Mix on medium speed until the dough comes together well—it will have the consistency of cookie dough.

6   To assemble the tart, grease the bottom and sides of a 9-inch cake pan with butter. Cut a 9-inch circle of parchment paper, and press it into the bottom of the pan. I prefer to use a piping bag to fill the pan with pastry, but you could simply use a rubber spatula. Fit a pastry bag with a plain tip that is about ½ inch in diameter. Scoop the pastry dough into the piping bag. Start piping rings of dough, starting in the center and working your way toward the edges. Cover the entire bottom of the pan. Then pipe another line of dough around the perimeter of the pan—this will create a wall where the custard will go.

7   Fill the center of the cavity with the custard, no higher than the top of the perimeter dough line, and smooth the top with a spatula. Do not overfill with custard or it will seep out the edges.

8   Finish piping the pastry dough over the custard, starting in the center and working your way to the edges of the pan.

9   Cover the tart with plastic wrap and gently press down to smooth the top. Refrigerate the tart until the pastry is firm, about 2 hours.

10   About 30 minutes before baking, preheat the oven to 350 degrees F. Beat the remaining egg, and brush it on the top of the pastry. Using a fork, create a crisscross pattern on top. Bake the tart for 50 to 60 minutes, until golden brown. Let the tart cool in the pan for at least 20 minutes as it has a tendency to crumble when hot. Turn the tart out onto a cooling rack, and let it rest for another 15 to 20 minutes before cutting. It can be stored in the refrigerator for up to 3 days.

One-Bowl Apricot and Olive Oil Cake

½ cup (115 g) extra-virgin olive oil, plus more for greasing pan
1 cup (140 g) superfine brown rice flour
¾ cup (150 g) granulated sugar
¾ cup (75 g) almond flour
¼ cup (30 g) tapioca starch
1½ teaspoons baking powder
½ teaspoon baking soda
½ teaspoon kosher salt
Finely grated zest of 1 lemon
½ cup (115 g) whole milk or almond milk (page 20)
2 large eggs
1 tablespoon vanilla extract
7 apricots, halved and pitted
2 tablespoons finely chopped pistachios
Powdered sugar, for dusting

This cake is what I refer to as a snack cake, mainly because I serve it to my children as an after-school treat or with a cup of coffee to friends that come by the studio. It is the easiest cake in my repertoire, only requiring a bowl and a whisk to mix. You can make it with any fruit you have on hand. It's wonderful with peaches, cherries, blueberries, or thinly sliced apples and pears. You can even make it without fruit (reduce baking time by 5 minutes) and use it as a simple cake for trifles or layered with cream.

I like to use fruity olive oil for this, such as arbequina, but you can use any kind you prefer.

MAKES ONE 9-INCH CAKE

1 Preheat the oven to 350 degrees F. Brush the bottom and sides of a 9-inch cake pan with olive oil and press a circle of parchment paper into the bottom.

2 In a large bowl, whisk together the brown rice flour, granulated sugar, almond flour, tapioca starch, baking powder, baking soda, salt, and lemon zest. Whisk in the olive oil, milk, eggs, and vanilla. Pour the batter into the prepared cake pan. Top the batter with the apricot halves, cut side up, overlapping them slightly.

3 Bake the cake for 60 to 70 minutes, or until golden brown and a toothpick inserted in the center comes out clean. Let the cake cool in the pan for 10 minutes, until cool enough to handle. Invert the cake onto a cooling rack and cool completely before serving with the chopped pistachios and a dusting of powdered sugar.

Apple Cider Yeast Doughnuts

2¼ cups (510 g) apple cider or unfiltered apple juice, heated to 105 degrees F

2 tablespoons (50 g) honey

4 teaspoons (15 g) active dry yeast

½ cup (115 g) unsalted or dairy-free butter, melted

3 tablespoons (30 g) psyllium husk powder

2 tablespoons (15 g) flaxseed meal

1 cup (120 g) tapioca starch

¾ cup (120 g) potato starch

¾ cup (105 g) superfine brown rice flour, plus more for dusting

¾ cup (105 g) sorghum flour

2 teaspoons kosher salt

2 teaspoons ground cinnamon, divided

Vegetable oil, for frying

½ cup (100 g) sugar

The smell of fried yeast doughnuts is incomparable and one that reminds me of Sunday morning farmers' markets. Because when the dark chill of the fall and winter months descends, one simply must have fried dough scented with apples and cinnamon. There's just no other way to make it through.

This recipe calls for apple cider—not the alcoholic, yeasty, murky cider I grew up with, but unfiltered and unpasteurized pressed apple juice. Apple cider is opaque, highly perishable, and contains more pulp than standard apple juice. Ideally you would get it at the apple orchard, but in a pinch, you can use unfiltered apple juice.

MAKES 14 DOUGHNUTS AND DOUGHNUT HOLES

1 Whisk together the apple cider, honey, and yeast in a large bowl. Proof for 10 minutes, until foamy. Whisk in the melted butter, psyllium powder, and flaxseed meal. Let the mixture gel for 5 minutes.

2 In the bowl of a stand mixer, combine the tapioca starch, potato starch, brown rice flour, sorghum flour, salt, and 1 teaspoon of the cinnamon. Give everything a good whisk, then add the yeast mixture. Mix the dough with a dough hook on medium speed for 3 minutes, until well incorporated. The dough will be sticky. Grease a large bowl and scrape the dough into it. Cover the bowl with plastic wrap or a clean kitchen towel and proof at room temperature for 1 hour, or until doubled. Place the bowl in the refrigerator, and chill the dough for 2 hours.

3 Fill a large Dutch oven with enough vegetable oil to be 3 inches deep. Place the pot over medium-high heat. Insert a heatproof candy thermometer, and continue heating until the oil reaches 375 degrees F. This will take a few minutes.

4 Mix the sugar and remaining ground cinnamon in a small bowl and set aside. Line a baking sheet with paper towels, and position it near the stovetop.

5   Dust a work surface with brown rice flour. Transfer the chilled dough onto the surface, dust the top with a bit more flour, then roll it into a ½-inch-thick rectangle. Dip a 2½-inch cookie cutter into brown rice flour and cut the doughnuts. Cut the holes using a 1-inch cutter. Roll the leftover dough one more time and cut it again—you should have about 14 doughnuts and holes. Discard the remaining dough.

6   Gently drop a few doughnuts into the oil, being careful not to splatter. Do not overcrowd the pot. The oil temperature will drop significantly when the doughnuts go in, so adjust the heat to maintain a 350-degree-F temperature. The doughnuts will sink to the bottom and rise back to the top after a few seconds. Cook the doughnuts for 2 to 3 minutes, carefully flip them, and cook for another 2 to 3 minutes. Lift out the doughnuts with a slotted spoon or spatula and drain on the paper towels. While they are still warm, dip them in the cinnamon sugar. Let the doughnuts rest for 10 minutes before feasting so the interior crumb sets, otherwise they might be a bit gummy while hot.

Roasted Squash Brown Butter Cake

The smell of spices and nutty brown butter that spreads through your kitchen while this cake bakes will turn your home into a space of cozy anticipation. You won't need a whole roasted squash for this cake, but I like to have abundant puree on hand for pies, other cakes, or soups, so I freeze the leftover and thaw it out in the refrigerator when I need it. I also bake mini cakes in decorative individual Bundt pans for my children. For this, I reduce the baking time by 10 minutes or so (do the toothpick test if you're unsure), then roll the cakes in cinnamon sugar.

MAKES 1 BUNDT CAKE

1 (2-pound or 1-kg) butternut squash or sugar pie pumpkin, halved lengthwise and seeded, or 1 cup (225 g) canned pumpkin
½ cup (110 g) unsalted butter, plus more for greasing the pan
1 cup (140 g) superfine brown rice flour
⅔ cup (65 g) almond flour
½ cup (100 g) granulated sugar
½ cup (100 g) light brown sugar
¼ cup (30 g) tapioca starch
¾ teaspoon kosher salt
½ teaspoon baking soda
½ teaspoon ground cinnamon
¼ teaspoon ground ginger
⅛ teaspoon ground nutmeg
3 eggs, lightly beaten, at room temperature
2 teaspoons finely grated orange zest
2 teaspoons freshly squeezed orange juice
Powdered sugar, for dusting

1 Preheat the oven to 400 degrees F.

2 Place the squash cut sides down on a baking sheet and bake for 45 minutes, or until the flesh is tender all the way through. Check by inserting the tip of a knife into the thickest part of the squash. Let the squash cool at room temperature until it can be handled. The skin should peel right off. Scoop the flesh into a blender or food processor and puree until smooth. Measure out 1 cup squash puree, and reserve the rest for another use. You could make soup with it or freeze it. Reduce the oven temperature to 350 degrees F.

3 Melt the butter in a small saucepan over medium-high heat. Continue cooking the butter until the milk solids start to turn brown and smell nutty. Pour the brown butter into a bowl and set aside to cool.

4 Brush the bottom and sides of a 6-cup Bundt pan with butter.

5 In a large bowl, whisk together the brown rice flour, almond flour, granulated and light brown sugars, tapioca starch, salt, baking soda, cinnamon, ginger, and nutmeg. Mix in the squash puree, cooled brown butter, eggs, orange zest, and orange juice until smooth.

6 Spoon the batter into the prepared Bundt pan. Bake for 40 to 45 minutes, or until golden brown and a toothpick inserted in the center of the cake comes out clean. Cool the cake in the pan for 10 minutes, then invert the cake onto a cooling rack and remove the pan. Let the cake cool for another 10 minutes, then dust the top with powdered sugar and serve. The cake will keep for 3 days wrapped in plastic at room temperature.

Banana Bread with Sunflower Seed Icing

This banana bread has been part of my repertoire since my pastry chef days, and it's the most requested cake from my children. The sunflower seed icing makes it even richer, although you can omit it. You could also use butter in the icing in place of coconut oil, which will give it a thicker texture.

MAKES 1 LOAF

1   Preheat the oven to 350 degrees F. Grease the bottom and sides of a one-pound loaf pan with olive oil and set aside. The cake has quite a bit of oil that may seep out, so don't overgrease the pan.

2   In a medium bowl, mash 3 of the bananas with a fork until there are some chunks left but it's fairly pureed. Add the granulated sugar, olive oil, eggs, ginger, and vanilla and mix until smooth.

3   In a large bowl, whisk together the almond flour, brown rice flour, salt, and baking soda. Pour in the banana mixture and stir until the batter comes together. Fold in the raw sunflower seeds.

4   Pour the batter into the loaf pan. Cut the remaining banana in half lengthwise and place on top of the batter. Sprinkle a few sunflower seeds on top of the cake and bake for 50 to 55 minutes, or until golden brown and a toothpick inserted in the center comes out clean. Set the pan on a cooling rack for 15 minutes, then invert the cake onto the rack and cool completely.

5   Reduce the oven temperature to 300 degrees F. Place the sunflower seeds for the icing on a baking sheet and bake for 10 minutes, until golden and fragrant. Set aside to cool completely.

6   In the bowl of a stand mixer, combine the sunflower butter and coconut oil. Beat on high speed with the whisk attachment until light, about 3 minutes. Add the powdered sugar and salt, then whisk again for another 3 minutes. Fold in the toasted sunflower seeds. The icing will be slightly liquid at this point, especially on warm days, so refrigerate until it sets, at least 1 hour.

7   Spread the sunflower seed icing over the top of the banana bread, or serve it on the side. The cake keeps in the refrigerator for 3 days, if you can wait that long.

For the banana bread

½ cup (115 g) extra-virgin olive oil or melted coconut oil, plus more for greasing

4 ripe medium bananas, peeled, divided

¾ cup (150 g) granulated sugar

3 large eggs

1 tablespoon finely grated peeled fresh ginger (optional)

2 teaspoons vanilla extract

1 cup (100 g) almond flour

¾ cup (105 g) superfine brown rice flour

½ teaspoon kosher salt

½ teaspoon baking soda

½ cup (75 g) raw sunflower seeds, plus more for topping

For the icing

⅓ cup (50 g) toasted sunflower seeds

½ cup (150 g) sunflower seed butter (page 28)

¼ cup (55 g) coconut oil or unsalted butter, at room temperature

½ cup (55 g) powdered sugar, sifted

½ teaspoon flaky sea salt

Flaky Caramelized Onion and Fennel Biscuits

½ cup (115 g) cultured butter (page 24), unsalted butter, or dairy-free butter

1 tablespoon extra-virgin olive oil

½ yellow onion, cut into ¼-inch dice (about ⅔ cup)

1 teaspoon fennel seeds

¾ teaspoon kosher salt, divided

½ cup plus 2 tablespoons (150 g) whole milk or almond milk (page 20)

2 tablespoons apple cider vinegar

½ cup (70 g) superfine brown rice flour, plus more for dusting

½ cup (60 g) tapioca starch

⅓ cup (60 g) potato starch

⅓ cup (50 g) sorghum flour

2¼ teaspoons baking powder

¼ teaspoon baking soda

¼ teaspoon xanthan gum

1 large egg, lightly beaten

1 teaspoon flaky sea salt

Years ago, when I was still eating gluten, I devoured Peter Reinhart's baking books. I referenced his techniques often and made his biscuits over and over again. This recipe for flaky biscuits takes from his idea of freezing and grating butter, and also gives the dough folds as you would with laminated doughs. The biscuits are savory and slightly sweet from the caramelized onions.

MAKES 8 BISCUITS

1   Preheat the oven to 500 degrees F. Line a baking sheet with parchment paper. Place the butter in the freezer for at least 30 minutes, or until frozen solid.

2   Heat the olive oil in a small saucepan over medium heat. Add the onion, fennel seeds, and ¼ teaspoon of the salt, and cook, stirring occasionally, until the onion is tender and slightly browned, about 7 minutes. Transfer the onion to a bowl and place in the freezer.

3   Combine the milk and apple cider vinegar in a small bowl, whisk together, and place in the freezer for 5 minutes.

4   In a large bowl, whisk together the brown rice flour, tapioca starch, potato starch, sorghum flour, baking powder, remaining ½ teaspoon salt, baking soda, and xanthan gum. Remove the butter from the freezer and grate it coarsely with a box grater. I do this directly over the flour to avoid handling it too long. The goal is to keep the butter as cold as possible for the entire process. Mix the grated butter into the flour using a wooden spoon. Add the chilled caramelized onions and milk mixture. Stir until combined. The dough will be sticky. Knead it with your hands for a few seconds to make sure it comes together into a mass.

5   Dust a work surface with brown rice flour. Transfer the dough onto the surface, and roll it into a rectangle that is three times as long as it is wide and about ½ inch thick. No need to be precise; it just needs to be folded like a letter. Fold one-third of the dough over the center third, then fold the other third over that. Rotate the dough 90 degrees, roll it into a rectangle again, and repeat the letter fold. Repeat a third ⟶

time, and flatten it into a rectangle that is about 8 inches by 4 inches. Measurements don't matter so much; you just want to cut even rectangle biscuits. Make sure the surface stays dusted with flour as you go along to keep the dough from sticking too much.

6 Using a sharp chef's knife, cut the dough in half lengthwise and then into quarters. I like to clean the blade after each cut, which helps to make nice clean cuts that will allow the biscuits to rise easier in the oven. You should have 8 rectangle biscuits. Place them on the baking sheet, brush the tops with the egg, and sprinkle with flaky sea salt.

7 Place the baking sheet in the oven, and reduce the temperature to 450 degrees F. Bake for 18 minutes, until golden brown. Transfer the baking sheet to a cooling rack, and let the biscuits cool on the pan for 5 minutes. Lift them off and serve immediately. They are best eaten while warm.

Strawberry Biscuits

Follow the same instructions on page 139, but omit the onion, fennel seeds, and olive oil, and reduce the kosher salt to ½ teaspoon.

At step 5, spread 2 tablespoons strawberry jam on the dough after rolling it out. Proceed with the letter folds. The jam might ooze out at the edges and become a bit messy; this is fine. You could also cut the dough into thirds and stack the layers instead.

Sprinkle the tops of the biscuits with a bit of coarse raw sugar instead of flaky salt once they have been brushed with egg. Bake as directed.

STEP 1

STEP 2

STEP 3

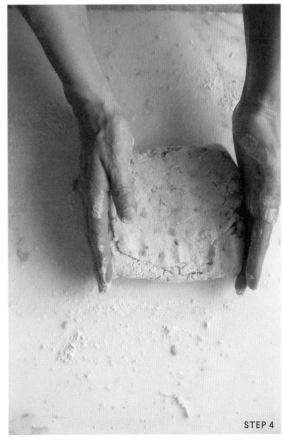

STEP 4

Parsnip and Ginger Cake with Cultured Butter and Crème Fraîche Icing

This cake is a variation on a traditional carrot cake but calls for the often underappreciated parsnip. The icing is a basic Swiss cream with the addition of tangy butter and crème fraîche, which really balances the sweetness of the cake.

MAKES ONE 8-INCH CAKE

1 Preheat the oven to 350 degrees F. Grease the bottom and sides of an 8-inch cake pan with olive oil. Cut out a circle of parchment paper, and press it into the bottom of the pan.

2 Grate the parsnip coarsely with a box grater. You should have approximately 1½ cups grated parsnip. Set aside.

3 Combine the brown sugar, ginger, and orange zest in a large bowl, then rub it between clean fingertips. This releases the flavor and oils of the ginger and orange zest. Whisk in the eggs and olive oil until smooth.

4 In a medium bowl, whisk together the almond flour, brown rice flour, tapioca starch, baking powder, and salt. Add this to the egg mixture and stir to combine. Fold in the grated parsnip and pour the batter into the cake pan.

5 Bake for 40 to 45 minutes, or until golden and a toothpick inserted in the center comes out clean. Place the cake pan on a cooling rack for 15 minutes, then invert the cake onto the rack to cool completely. The cake should be cool prior to icing.

6 While the cake cools, make the icing. Bring a small pot of water to a simmer over medium heat. Combine the egg whites and sugar in the bowl of stand mixer, and whisk together until smooth. Place the bowl above the simmering water, and continue whisking until the sugar has melted and the whites are hot to the touch and very marshmallow-like. Bring the bowl back to the mixer and whip on high speed with the whisk attachment. The whites will triple in volume and release a lot of steam. Continue whipping until the whites are thick and the bowl feels cool to the touch, about 7 minutes. It's important to wait until the egg whites are cool before proceeding to the next step or the butter will melt.

For the cake

½ cup (125 g) extra-virgin olive oil, plus more for greasing

1 large (5 ounces or 150 g) parsnip, peeled

¾ cup (150 g) light brown sugar

3 tablespoons finely grated peeled fresh ginger

1 tablespoon finely grated orange zest

3 large eggs

¾ cup (75 g) almond flour

½ cup (70 g) superfine brown rice flour

2 tablespoons (15 g) tapioca starch

1½ teaspoons baking powder

½ teaspoon kosher salt

For the icing

2 egg whites

½ cup (100 g) sugar

10 tablespoons (150 g) cultured
butter (page 24), at room
temperature

2 tablespoons (30 g) crème
fraîche (page 26)

1 teaspoon vanilla extract

¼ cup hazelnuts, toasted and
coarsely chopped

7   With the mixer running on medium speed, add 1 tablespoon
of the soft butter at a time. Wait a few seconds between butter
additions. Once all the butter has been added, turn speed back
up to high and whip for 1 minute to ensure all the butter is well
integrated and aerated. Fold in the crème fraîche and vanilla.

8   Using a spatula, spread the icing on top of the cooled
parsnip cake. Sprinkle the hazelnuts on top and serve. The cake
can be kept wrapped with plastic in the refrigerator for up to
3 days.

CHAPTER FOUR

Midday

Growing up in the Basque Country, lunch was always the main meal of the day. At school, we took a two-hour break to go home and eat lunch with our families, then returned to finish our lessons. While both of my parents worked outside the home, we always gathered for lunch. Shops closed between two o'clock and four o'clock, the streets became vacant, and the only sounds to be heard were the clicking of plates and glasses, the echo of chairs being dragged to the table, and the murmur of families as they reconnected at the day's midpoint. Those sounds are clear in my mind and indicated a communal time to slow down, nourish our bodies, converse, and then rest. Sadly, the culture of a big lunch and a siesta are no longer part of my weekday routine, but I still make time for a light and nourishing lunch.

I often invite friends and colleagues to my studio for an impromptu midday meal. They gather around the kitchen island while I chop, sauté, and stir. I keep the mood light and casual. Most of the time, they sit, I stand. I serve lunch on mismatched vintage and handmade plates. Recipes are simple and uncomplicated, which allows me to engage in the conversation—roasted carrot and cashew soup; chicken salad with apples, celery, and pickles; or one of my favorite Basque-inspired dishes, sautéed mushrooms and eggs. I make a pot of French press coffee with coconut milk and offer a sliver of chocolate as a sweet ending.

These short visits fill me with joy and allow me to honor some elements of the lunch rituals I grew up with. While lunchtime can't always be a time for community and connection, it can serve as a vital break from the flow of the day. It's an opportunity to change the energy, and creating that space will fill you with the verve needed to be both alert and mindful into the evening hours.

Winter Salad with Roasted Radicchio, Avocados, and Hazelnut Dukkah

4 medium golden beets, trimmed

2 heads radicchio

6 tablespoons extra-virgin olive oil, divided

1½ teaspoons flaky sea salt, divided

½ teaspoon freshly ground black pepper

2 medium oranges, zested, peeled, and thinly sliced

2 medium avocados, peeled, pitted, and sliced

1 tablespoon honey (preferably raw and local)

1 tablespoon apple cider vinegar

1 teaspoon whole-grain mustard

½ Fresno chili, seeded and finely chopped

¼ cup hazelnut dukkah (page 40) or coarsely chopped toasted hazelnuts

¼ cup sprouts, such as radish, broccoli, or any microgreen

I love the combination of bitter and sweet, which makes this salad one of my favorite wintertime lunches. Radicchio's bitterness is tamed when roasted, and when it's paired with sweet beets, oranges, and avocado, it makes a wonderfully balanced and bright salad.

MAKES 4 SERVINGS

1 Preheat the oven to 400 degrees F.

2 Wrap the beets in foil, place them on a baking sheet, and bake until tender, about 40 minutes. Check doneness by sticking the tip of a knife into the center of a beet to see if it slides in easily.

3 Meanwhile, prepare the radicchio. Cut each head in half, then cut each half into thirds, keeping the core intact so the leaves stay together. Place the radicchio on a baking sheet and brush the cut sides with 2 tablespoons of the olive oil and sprinkle with 1 teaspoon of the salt and the pepper. Position the radicchio so that one of the cut edges rests directly on the baking sheet. Roast for 15 minutes, rotating the pan once. The radicchio will be tender with caramelized edges. Set aside.

4 When the beets are done cooking, carefully unwrap the foil and wait a few minutes until they are cool enough to handle. Peel and quarter them.

5 Arrange the radicchio, beets, orange slices, and avocados on a platter.

6 In a small bowl, whisk together the remaining 4 tablespoons olive oil, orange zest, honey, vinegar, mustard, chili, and remaining ½ teaspoon salt. Drizzle the dressing over the salad and top with the dukkah and sprouts.

Spicy Chicken Salad with Apple, Celery, and Pickled Vegetables

Leftovers are the foundation of my lunches, and roasted chicken is the dish that keeps on giving. I like the slight sweet and sour flavors in this salad, along with the crunch of all the elements. Giving the chicken a little caramelization and crispness makes this version very flavorful and more complex than your typical chicken salad. I call for pickled fennel and red onion, but any pickled vegetables will work because their role is to add acidity and crunch.

MAKES 4 SERVINGS

1 Combine the chicken, olive oil, and chili paste in a bowl and toss until all the chicken is coated. Heat a medium sauté pan over medium-high heat, add the chicken, and cook until the edges are crispy on all sides, about 5 minutes. Chili paste often has sugar in it, making it tend to burn, so watch the heat. Transfer the chicken to a serving bowl, and let it cool for a couple of minutes.

2 Add the apples, celery, vinegar, salt, and pepper to the bowl and toss to combine. Top the salad with cashews, pickled vegetables, parsley, mint, and tarragon, then drizzle the top with more olive oil. Serve immediately.

- 12 ounces (340 g) leftover roasted chicken (see Note), shredded into bite-size pieces
- 3 tablespoons extra-virgin olive oil, plus more for drizzling
- 2 tablespoons chili paste or spicy harissa (see Note)
- 2 medium Granny Smith apples, quartered and thinly sliced crosswise
- 3 stalks celery, thinly sliced
- 1 tablespoon red wine vinegar
- ½ teaspoon flaky sea salt
- ½ teaspoon freshly ground black pepper
- ½ cup (75 g) roasted cashews, coarsely chopped
- ¼ cup pickled fennel and red onion (see page 44)
- ¼ cup Italian parsley leaves, tough stems removed and leaves torn
- ¼ cup mint leaves, tough stems removed and leaves torn
- ¼ cup tarragon leaves, tough stems removed and leaves torn

Note: If you don't have any leftover roasted chicken, simply rub 2 bone-in, skin-on chicken thighs with olive oil, salt, and pepper; place on a small baking sheet; and roast at 425 degrees F for about 25 minutes, or until the internal temperature is 165 degrees F. If you don't have chili paste or harissa on hand, rub the chicken with 1 teaspoon chili powder and ½ teaspoon honey, and increase the olive oil to 5 tablespoons.

Buttermilk-Poached Salmon Salad with Herb, Leek, and Caper Dressing

1 pound (450 g) skinless wild
    salmon, cut into 2 equal pieces
1 teaspoon kosher salt
1 small leek (white part only),
    halved lengthwise and cut into
    ½-inch slices
2 cups (225 g) full-fat buttermilk
1 cup (115 g) cold water
1 medium lemon, zested and juiced
2 tablespoons capers, chopped
2 tablespoons extra-virgin
    olive oil
1 tablespoon finely chopped
    tarragon
1 tablespoon finely chopped dill
1 tablespoon finely chopped
    chives
1 teaspoon grainy mustard
2 bunches baby romaine, or
    1 large romaine head, leaves
    torn into large pieces
¼ cup whole or pitted
    Castelvetrano olives
¼ cup pickled shallots
    (page 44), optional
3 tablespoons coarsely
    chopped pistachios

There is something about fatty salmon that pairs nicely with acid, salt, and the allium family. In this recipe, the salmon is slowly poached in a mixture of buttermilk and leeks until very tender, then served with the classics: capers, olives, pickles, and lots of tender herbs. Select pieces of salmon that are not too thick so they cook evenly and all the way through.

MAKES 4 SERVINGS

1   Season both sides of the salmon with the salt. Place the salmon and leeks in a large skillet and cover with the buttermilk, water, and lemon juice. Bring the liquid to a simmer over medium heat, cover the pan, remove it from the heat, and let it sit for 15 to 18 minutes, depending on salmon thickness, until it is tender and slightly pink in the center. The poaching liquid might curdle slightly and that is OK. Using a slotted spatula, transfer the salmon and leeks to a clean plate. Break the salmon into bite-size pieces with a fork. Coarsely chop the leeks.

2   Measure ½ cup of the buttermilk poaching liquid into a bowl. Whisk in the leeks, capers, olive oil, tarragon, dill, chives, mustard, and lemon zest.

3   Toss together the romaine, olives, shallots, pistachios, and salmon on a platter and drizzle with the dressing. Taste and adjust the salt if needed. Serve immediately.

Shaved Beet and Lentil Salad with Tahini and Preserved Lemon Dressing

2½ cups (565 g) cold water
1 cup (200 g) French lentils,
  rinsed in cold water
2 large cloves garlic, peeled
  and crushed
2 thyme sprigs
¼ cup extra-virgin olive oil,
  divided
2 teaspoons coriander seeds
1 teaspoon cumin seeds
2 tablespoons tahini
2 tablespoons finely chopped
  preserved lemon rinds
  (page 48)
2 tablespoons apple cider vinegar
1 tablespoon finely chopped
  Italian parsley
1 teaspoon flaky sea salt
½ teaspoon freshly ground
  black pepper
2 medium golden beets, peeled
  and thinly sliced
2 medium Chioggia beets,
  peeled and thinly sliced
2 radishes, thinly sliced
½ small red onion, thinly sliced

This salad is hearty and earthy. The nuttiness of beets, tahini, and lentils is balanced by the briny preserved lemons. Lentils are my go-to legume for soups and salads. They don't require soaking, and they cook relatively quickly. A time-saving tip: When you cook lentils for this salad, make a double batch and freeze half for another time. Store in a tightly sealed freezer storage bag for up to 3 months. To thaw, simply fill a large bowl with hot water and submerge the plastic bag in it until the lentils are thawed out, about 15 minutes.

MAKES 4 SERVINGS

1   Combine water, lentils, garlic, thyme, and 2 tablespoons of the olive oil in a medium pot over medium-high heat. Cover, reduce heat to medium low, bring to a simmer, and cook until the lentils are tender, 30 to 35 minutes. Pick out the garlic and thyme and discard. Drain any excess liquid, and transfer the lentils to a large bowl.

2   Meanwhile, toast the coriander and cumin seeds in a small dry skillet over medium heat until fragrant, about 2 minutes. Transfer to a mortar and pestle and grind to a powder. Transfer to a small bowl and whisk in the remaining 2 tablespoons olive oil, tahini, preserved lemon, vinegar, parsley, salt, and pepper. Pour the dressing over the lentils and toss to combine. Add the beets and toss again. Top with the radishes and red onion and serve immediately.

Simple Asparagus and Avocado Soup

2 tablespoons unsalted butter

1 medium leek (white and very light-green parts only), finely chopped

1 teaspoon kosher salt, divided

1 pound (454 g) green asparagus, trimmed and cut into ½-inch pieces

3 cups (100 g) chopped greens, such as spinach, mustard greens, ramp greens, or nettles

4 cups (800 g) vegetable stock (page 56)

1 ripe medium avocado, peeled and pitted

Juice of 1 lemon

¼ cup (55 g) whole-milk yogurt (page 32) or canned full-fat coconut milk

Finely chopped chives, for garnish

This soup takes literally fifteen minutes to make, and it is rich, silky, and filled with all the goodness of spring. Serve it plain or with toasted hazelnuts and soft-cooked eggs as suggested. Other toppings could be smoked salmon with dill and capers, crispy chickpeas (page 188) and pepitas, or roasted cauliflower (page 192).

MAKES 4 SERVINGS

1 Melt the butter in a large pot over medium heat. Add the leeks and ½ teaspoon of the salt. Stir and cook for 5 minutes, or until tender. Add the asparagus, greens, and the remaining ½ teaspoon salt. Stir the vegetables for 30 seconds, then add the stock. Cover the pot, bring to a simmer, and cook for 5 minutes, or until all the vegetables are tender.

2 Transfer the soup to a blender (in batches as needed), and add the avocado. Puree until smooth, being sure to let steam escape. Add the lemon juice, stir, then taste the soup one more time to adjust the seasoning.

3 Top the soup with the yogurt and chives. Serve immediately.

Roasted Carrot and Cashew Soup

I love a good pureed vegetable soup. They are creamy and simple, and then get topped with some crunchy bits and paired with dark, toasted bread for a satiating meal. Because the roasted carrots are so sweet, this soup needs all of the listed spices, as well as the acidity from lime juice or vinegar, for balance.

MAKES 6 SERVINGS

2 pounds (1 kg) carrots, scrubbed and cut into 2-inch pieces

4 cloves garlic, peeled and crushed

1 medium shallot, quartered

3 tablespoons coconut or extra-virgin olive oil, plus more for drizzling

1 teaspoon kosher salt

1 teaspoon freshly ground black pepper

1 teaspoon ground coriander

½ teaspoon ground sumac, plus more for garnish

½ teaspoon red pepper flakes

6 cups (675 g) vegetable stock (page 56)

½ cup (80 g) raw cashews, divided

½ cup (115 g) unsweetened cashew milk (page 20) or coconut milk (page 21)

2 tablespoons freshly squeezed lime juice or apple cider vinegar

1 Preheat the oven to 400 degrees F. Place the carrots in a large bowl with the garlic, shallot, olive oil, salt, black pepper, coriander, sumac, and red pepper flakes. Toss everything together and transfer to a baking sheet large enough for the carrots to fit in a single layer. Bake for 30 to 40 minutes, or until tender.

2 Meanwhile, heat the vegetable stock in a saucepan over low heat and keep warm.

3 Toast the cashews in a small dry skillet until fragrant, then transfer ¼ cup of them to a high-speed blender, reserving the rest for garnish. Add the cashew milk and puree.

4 Puree the soup in two batches if necessary, combining about half the stock, carrots, and cashew puree in each batch and stirring everything together again before serving. Taste the soup and adjust the seasoning if needed. Add the lime juice, give the soup one last blend, and serve immediately while warm. Top with the remaining ¼ cup toasted cashews, drizzle with olive oil, and sprinkle with a little sumac.

Peas and Ham with Buttermilk Dressing

Come spring, I run to the farmers' market for the first shelling peas and the sweetest sugar snap peas. It signifies the beginning of the abundance that is to come. My mother made *guisantes con jamón* (peas with ham) for herself nearly once a week when the season came around. It was her favorite dish, with some chopped hard-cooked egg on top. My version is different than hers, but it plays with similar flavors of sweet and salty with the added tang from the buttermilk dressing. This dish is super vibrant and comes together in an instant.

MAKES 4 SERVINGS

1 pound (454 g) English peas, shelled

8 ounces (225 g) sugar snap peas, thinly sliced lengthwise

1 cup watercress

¼ cup basil leaves

2 tablespoons finely chopped chives

½ teaspoon flaky sea salt

½ teaspoon freshly ground black pepper

2 tablespoons extra-virgin olive oil, plus more for drizzling

1 spring garlic, or 3 cloves garlic, thinly sliced

4 large thin slices serrano or Ibérico ham or prosciutto

½ cup (115 g) full-fat buttermilk

½ cup (115 g) whole-milk yogurt (page 32)

1 medium lemon, zested and juiced

1   Bring a pot of water to a boil over high heat. Salt the water generously, as if you were cooking pasta. Add the English peas and boil until just tender, about 2 minutes. Drain in a colander and run under cold water. Transfer to a large bowl along with the sugar snap peas, watercress, basil, chives, salt, and pepper and toss to combine.

2   Heat the olive oil in a small sauté pan over medium heat. Add the garlic and cook until golden. Add the ham and cook for 30 seconds on each side, or until slightly crispy. Pour the oil with garlic and ham onto a plate, and let it cool while you prepare the dressing.

3   Whisk together the buttermilk, yogurt, and lemon juice and zest in a small bowl. Pour the dressing into the bottom of a large bowl or divide among four plates. Top with the pea mixture, then sprinkle the garlic and drizzle olive oil all over it. Break the ham into bite-size pieces and scatter over the top. Finish with more salt, pepper, and olive oil if needed. Serve immediately.

Melon, Serrano, Fennel, and Ricotta Salata

Melon and serrano are one of summer's quintessential pairings, and these flavors often began our family meals in August. Our day trips took us on longs walks through the forest, enjoying a picnic in a vast meadow. We would gather together after purchasing the ripest green melons on the side of the road. My mother unwrapped a perfect package of Ibérico ham that she got at the *charcutero* the morning of, then wrapped each wedge of melon with the salty, slightly oily, paper-thin piece of cured pork. I am not even sure if this can be classified as a salad or more of an arranged plate with strong components that are drizzled with olive oil, but no matter what you call it, it's wonderful.

MAKES 4 SERVINGS

1 small green melon, such as honeydew, peeled, seeded, and cut into wedges

8 thin slices serrano ham (*speck* or prosciutto will work if that's all you can find)

1 medium fennel bulb, thinly sliced (reserve some fronds for garnish)

6-ounce (170-g) block ricotta salata, broken into large pieces

2 tablespoons extra-virgin olive oil

1 medium lemon

¼ cup chopped pistachios or dukkah (page 40), optional

1   Arrange the melon on a platter. Wrap the serrano around the melon pieces. Scatter the fennel and ricotta around the platter. Drizzle everything with olive oil. Finely grate the lemon zest over the salad, then halve it and squeeze the lemon juice all over it. Top with the pistachios and serve immediately.

Tomato, Corn, and Bread Salad

When summer rolls around, I can survive on sliced ripe tomatoes served with a thick, toasted slice of sourdough bread to soak up all the tomato juice. That's how the traditional *panzanella* salad came to be, and this version is a variation of the classic with sweet corn and some pickled radishes for acidity. I love using a variety of heirloom and Green Zebra tomatoes for their different sizes, shapes, and colors.

MAKES 4 SERVINGS

3 slices Sourdough Boules (page 103) or other bread of choice

5 tablespoons extra-virgin olive oil, divided

2 teaspoons flaky sea salt, divided

½ teaspoon freshly ground black pepper

2 pounds (1 kg) ripe tomatoes, such as heirloom or Green Zebra

2 ears of fresh corn, husks removed and kernels cut

⅓ cup pickled radishes (page 44)

¼ cup fresh tender herbs, such as basil, dill, marjoram, chives, or parsley

1 clove garlic, peeled and grated

½ Fresno chili, seeded and finely chopped

1   Preheat the oven to 350 degrees F. Tear the bread into bite-size pieces and toss together with 2 tablespoons of the olive oil, 1 teaspoon of the salt, and the black pepper on a baking sheet. Bake for 15 minutes, or until toasted.

2   Cut and slice the tomatoes into different shapes and mix with the remaining 1 teaspoon salt in a large bowl. Let sit for 10 minutes—the salt will draw water out from the tomatoes and intensify their flavor. Add the toasted bread and gently toss together so the bread can soak up the tomato water. Let sit for another 5 minutes.

3   Add the corn kernels, pickled radishes, herbs, garlic, chili, and remaining 3 tablespoons olive oil and toss to combine. Serve immediately.

Mushrooms and Eggs

1 pound (454 g) assorted
    mushrooms (chanterelles,
    morels, oysters, creminis)
2 tablespoons extra-virgin olive
    oil, plus more for frying
2 cloves garlic, smashed
2 sprigs thyme
1 teaspoon flaky sea salt
1 tablespoon salted butter or
    cultured butter (page 24)
1 tablespoon apple cider vinegar
2 teaspoons grainy Dijon mustard
1 tablespoon finely chopped
    Italian parsley
4 large eggs
4 slices Nordic Rye-Style Seed
    Bread (page 101) or other bread
    of choice, toasted

My father is an avid mushroom forager, just as his father, brother, and uncles were. In his car you will find a wicker basket, a pocket knife tightly knotted around the basket's handle, rain boots, and a long wooden stick he takes into the forest with him whenever he senses mushrooms might pop up. In the spring and early fall, he monitors the rainfall and warmth to estimate when he might be able to go out into the woods to collect porcinis, chanterelles, or *gibelurdinak* (*Russula virescens*)—one of his favorites and most coveted. It is usually a daylong affair for him—sometimes a friend or two might tag along, but most of the time it is a meditative, solitary hike. On fruitful trips, he returns home proud with a basketful that he shares with friends and family. He cleans the mushrooms carefully and meticulously by removing dirt with a dry pastry brush. Never does he run the mushrooms under water. He sautés them in a pan simply with olive oil, garlic, and salt until they begin to caramelize and get tender, then finishes them with a sprinkle of parsley. It's one of my life's greatest pleasures to join him on these hikes whenever I can, and this recipe is an homage to him.

MAKES 4 SERVINGS

1   Clean any dirt from the mushrooms using a pastry brush or a dry towel. Chop the mushrooms into 2-inch pieces and if they are small, leave them whole. Heat a large cast-iron pan over medium-high heat. Add the olive oil, garlic, and thyme, and cook for 1 minute to flavor the oil. Add the mushrooms, stir, and cook until caramelized, about 10 minutes. They will have some bite yet be tender. Season with the salt and stir again. Add the butter, vinegar, and mustard. Stir once more, and let reduce for 1 minute until creamy. Remove the pan from the heat, and stir in the parsley.

2   Heat a sauté pan over high heat. Add a splash of oil and fry the eggs two at a time until the whites are crispy and the yolks are still runny. Serve the eggs with the mushrooms and the toasted bread.

Crunchy Romaine Salad with Soft Eggs and Feta

There is nothing more satisfying than the contrast of a crunchy salad with some luxurious, creamy elements. Here, the crunch of romaine is balanced with the silky texture of avocado, soft feta, and creamy egg yolk. I specify Little Gem lettuce on the ingredient list as an alternative to the easier-to-find romaine. Usually Little Gems are only available at farmers' markets, but they are worth seeking out for their sweet and tender leaves.

MAKES 4 SERVINGS

4 large eggs
2 medium lemons
2 heads baby romaine (Little Gem), or 1 large head romaine, outer leaves removed and washed
2 medium avocados
7 ounces (190 g) sheep's milk feta (preferably block, not crumbles)
½ medium cucumber, thinly sliced
4 radishes, thinly sliced
½ cup sprouts or microgreens
⅓ cup (75 g) extra-virgin olive oil
1 teaspoon whole-grain mustard
1 clove garlic, finely minced
½ teaspoon flaky sea salt
½ teaspoon freshly ground black pepper

1   Fill a small pot with water and bring to a boil. Fill a medium bowl with ice water. Gently lower the eggs into the boiling water and cook for 7 minutes. Transfer them to the ice water until they are completely cooled, about 5 minutes. Peel the eggs, then halve lengthwise. Set aside.

2   Quarter one of the lemons. Divide the romaine among four large plates. Cut the avocados in half lengthwise, and with a spoon, scoop out bite-size pieces onto the romaine. Crumble the feta into bite-size chunks. Top the romaine with the cucumber, radishes, feta, sprouts, a lemon wedge, and an egg.

3   Zest and juice the remaining lemon. In a small bowl, whisk together the olive oil, lemon juice and zest, mustard, garlic, salt, and pepper. Pour over the salads and serve immediately.

Black Rice Bowl with Figs, Radicchio, Pickled Radishes, and Pepitas

There are so many reasons why I love black rice—the rich dark purple or black color, its balance of chewiness and tenderness, and its nutty sweetness complemented by an umami briny flavor that, while difficult to explain, is somehow unmistakable. It pairs really well with the sweet figs and bitter greens. Because figs have such short season, you can substitute with apples, pears, or even roasted grapes. It's a hearty bowl, for sure.

MAKES 4 SERVINGS

1 To make the candied pepitas, first lay a sheet of parchment paper on a work surface. Place the pepitas in a medium sauté pan over medium-high heat. Stir constantly and cook until they begin to toast, about 5 minutes. Sprinkle with the sugar, salt, cumin, and cayenne and stir. Continue cooking, stirring constantly, until the sugar has melted and coats the pepitas, about 3 minutes. The sugar can quickly burn, so reduce the heat if needed. Immediately spread the candied pepitas in an even layer over the parchment paper and let them cool—they will become crunchy. The pepitas can be stored in airtight container for up to 1 week.

2 To cook the rice, heat 1 tablespoon of the olive oil a small saucepan over medium heat. Add the rice and cook, stirring, for 1 minute. Add the water and ½ teaspoon of the salt, cover the pan, reduce the heat to low, and cook for 25 minutes, or until the rice is al dente.

3 To compose the dish, first stir together the labneh, cumin, coriander, and remaining ½ teaspoon salt in a small bowl. Spoon 2 tablespoons of the mixture into each of 4 bowls and spread it all around with the back of the spoon. Layer in the black rice, radicchio, pepitas, pickled radishes, and figs. Drizzle the remaining 2 tablespoons olive oil over the figs, sprinkled with a pinch of sumac, and serve immediately.

For the candied pepitas
½ cup (70 g) pepitas (pumpkin seeds)
2 teaspoons sugar
¼ teaspoon kosher salt
¼ teaspoon ground cumin
⅛ teaspoon cayenne

For the rice bowl
1 cup (200 g) black rice (often called forbidden rice)
3 tablespoons extra-virgin olive oil, divided
2 cups (450 g) cold water
1 teaspoon kosher salt, divided
½ cup (115 g) labneh (page 37) or whole-milk Greek-style yogurt
1 teaspoon ground cumin
1 teaspoon ground coriander
1 radicchio, halved, cored, and thinly sliced
½ cup pickled radishes (page 44)
8 figs, quartered
Pinch of sumac (optional)

CHAPTER FIVE

Everyday Dinners

While the wee morning hours are dedicated to solo quiet time, the evenings are about connecting with my family. There's an intimacy around the dinner table that I cherish, and the act of creating and sharing food is the conduit for conversations I crave with my husband and two children. Like so many things, weekday dinners provide me balance. There is also a twofold value to dinnertime—it's both utilitarian in its necessity and transformative in terms of our relationships.

Weeknights also contain a certain liveliness. The household buzzes with children underfoot, and the clutter of the day spills between rooms. These hectic evenings call for ease. I often fall into the well-worn patterns that have been etched into my cooking muscle memory, creating meals reflective of my mother's kitchen: chicken with apple cider vinegar or thick Spanish tortillas are staples. Because time is so often the greatest limitation, planning and preparing menus in advance can make execution a no-brainer.

The recipes in this chapter are meant to help you get a nourishing meal on the table quickly, and they don't require an abundance of attention. Baking for thirty minutes gives you half an hour to help with homework. Stewing on the stovetop means a few extra minutes to catch up with your spouse or give your pet some love.

I would be naïve if I encouraged you to cook these meals on busy weeknights and didn't acknowledge the bit of planning that I believe should take place prior. Every Sunday morning, I make a list of meals for the week and spend a bit of time sorting through the ingredients that are already at home, seeing how to best use them up first. Then I head to the farmers' market, followed by a trip to the supermarket, to stock up my fridge and pantry for the week. If there is any bit of prep to do for the week, such as making stocks, yogurt, or granola, I do that on Sundays. It feels extremely grounding to set the intention for the week to come.

Roasted Carrots with Red Lentil Hummus

I have been making hummus for years, but it was Heidi Swanson's *Near & Far* that introduced me to the use of red lentils in place of chickpeas. It's a brilliant approach because red lentils require no soaking and take 15 minutes to cook. You may be surprised to see that once the cooked lentils are mixed with the rest of the ingredients, the hummus is light and pale in color. I love the pairing of the hummus with the roasted vegetables and topped with crunchy pine nuts. I serve this dish often at larger gatherings too because it's easy to multiply for a crowd. The leftovers are always great the next day. Serve with a salad of Peppery Greens with Mustard-Honey Vinaigrette (page 240).

MAKES 4 SERVINGS

For the red lentil hummus
1 cup (185 g) red lentils
1½ cups plus 2 tablespoons
   (360 g) cold water
2 cloves garlic, peeled
⅓ cup (120 g) tahini
1½ teaspoons fine sea salt
½ teaspoon freshly ground black
   pepper
½ teaspoon ground cumin
⅓ cup (75 g) freshly squeezed
   lemon juice (from 2 or 3 lemons)
¼ cup (55 g) extra-virgin olive oil

For the roasted carrots
1 pound (454 g) baby carrots (if
   using larger carrots, peel, halve,
   and cut into 2-inch pieces)
½ medium red onion, cut into
   ½-inch wedges
¼ cup (55 g) extra-virgin olive oil
1 teaspoon ground cumin
1 teaspoon sumac (optional)
1 teaspoon kosher salt
½ teaspoon freshly ground
   black pepper
½ cup (70 g) pine nuts

1   Preheat the oven to 425 degrees F.

2   To make the hummus, rinse the lentils in a fine-mesh sieve under cold water until the water runs clear. Shake them around and remove any debris you find. Transfer the lentils to a small saucepan with 1½ cups of the water, cover, and bring to a simmer over medium-high heat. Reduce the heat to low and cook for 10 to 15 minutes, or until the red lentils are tender and the water has been absorbed. The lentils can be cooked ahead of time and refrigerated in an airtight container for up to 2 days. However, they do dry out a bit, so you may need to add a couple tablespoons of warm water when processing the hummus.

3   Transfer the lentils to a food processor with the garlic and process for about 3 minutes, or until creamy and smooth. Scrape the sides well, then add the tahini, salt, pepper, and cumin. Process for another 3 minutes. It's important to process for this long because it incorporates air into the hummus and makes it very creamy. At this point the hummus will be thick. Scrape the sides one more time. With the machine running, slowly drizzle in the lemon juice, olive oil, and remaining 2 tablespoons water. Scrape the sides one last time, taste, and adjust the seasoning if needed. Pulse a couple more times,

then transfer to a clean bowl. The hummus will be loose and creamy. You should have about 3 cups. It can be used right away or stored in the refrigerator for up to 3 days; first coat the top with olive oil, which will prevent a skin from forming, then cover the bowl with plastic wrap. I like to serve the hummus at room temperature, so I take it out a couple of hours before serving.

4   While the lentils are cooking, roast the carrots. Toss the carrots, onion, olive oil, cumin, sumac, salt, and pepper on a baking sheet, making sure all the carrots are coated with oil and spices. Bake for 20 to 25 minutes, until caramelized and tender. Note that sometimes when carrots are a bit tough, they take a while to bake and can easily burn on the outside while still being too firm on the inside. To avoid this, when the exteriors are caramelized, turn off the oven and leave the pan inside for another 15 minutes. The carrots will continue to cook at a lower temperature and have a chance to soften without burning.

5   Place the pine nuts in a dry sauté pan over medium heat and toast, tossing frequently, until they begin to darken, about 3 minutes. Transfer to a small bowl.

6   To serve, spoon 2 heaping tablespoons hummus on each plate and top with roasted carrots and toasted pine nuts. Drizzle some of the olive oil from the sheet pan over the top and serve.

Tomato and Romesco Tart

Romesco is a classic Spanish sauce made with almonds, bell peppers, and tomatoes. It is creamy and rich and a great complement to roasted vegetables, fish, eggs, chicken, or pork. When I have some left over, I love slathering it over toasted bread and topping it with a fried egg. It's absolute heaven.

This is one of my favorite tarts in the summer when tomatoes of all shapes and colors are abundant. If possible, choose meatier tomatoes with less water content so the pastry doesn't become too soggy—beefsteaks, Brandywine, Cherokee Purple, and Green Zebra are some of my favorites. You can make this tart using store-bought pastry sheets, which are really convenient.

MAKES 4 SERVINGS

For the romesco
½ cup (75 g) whole almonds, coarsely chopped
1 clove garlic, peeled
2 pieces roasted red bell pepper (jarred or homemade)
2 tablespoons tomato sauce
2 tablespoons red wine vinegar
1 tablespoon finely chopped Italian parsley
1 teaspoon Spanish *pimentón de la Vera* or smoked paprika
½ teaspoon kosher salt
¼ teaspoon cayenne
½ cup (115 g) extra-virgin olive oil

For the tart
Superfine brown rice flour, for dusting
½ recipe puff pastry (page 119)
2 pounds (1 kg) ripe yet firm tomatoes, thinly sliced
1 tablespoon fresh oregano, or 1 teaspoon dried
1 teaspoon flaky sea salt
½ teaspoon freshly ground black pepper
1 large egg, lightly beaten

1   Preheat the oven to 425 degrees F. Line a sheet pan with parchment paper.

2   To make the romesco, combine the almonds and garlic in a food processor and pulse until finely ground, about 2 minutes. Add the bell pepper, tomato sauce, vinegar, parsley, pimentón, salt, and cayenne and process until smooth, about 1 minute. Scrape the sides of the bowl, then steadily drizzle in the olive oil with the machine running. You should have about 1¼ cups romesco, which is more than you will need for the tart. Measure out ½ cup, and transfer the remaining romesco to a sealed jar. It can be stored in the refrigerator for up to 1 week.

3   To make the tart, dust a work surface with brown rice flour and roll out the puff pastry to ⅛ inch thick. Transfer it to the sheet pan. Spoon the reserved ½ cup romesco into the center of the pastry, then spread it out toward the edges of the dough, leaving a 1-inch border. Arrange the sliced tomatoes over the sauce, lightly overlapping. Sprinkle with the oregano, salt, and pepper, then fold the dough edges over the tomatoes, pinching any cracked edges. If your dough feels soft, refrigerate the tart for 15 minutes.

4   Brush the pastry edges with the beaten egg. Bake for 40 to 45 minutes, until the tomatoes are bubbling and the crust is golden brown. Cool for 5 minutes before cutting into wedges.

My Niçoise Salad

---

4 large eggs

1 pound (454 g) baby purple or red potatoes, halved if large

12 ounces (340 g) haricots verts

5 tablespoons extra-virgin olive oil, divided

1 tablespoon capers, drained and patted dry with a paper towel

2 tablespoons red wine vinegar

2 teaspoons Dijon mustard

2 tablespoons finely chopped dill sprigs, plus more for garnish

1 teaspoon flaky sea salt

3 cups mixed greens

8 ounces (225 g) bonito tuna packed in olive oil, drained

8 ounces (225 g) grape tomatoes, halved

2 avocados, peeled, pitted, and quartered

4 ounces (115 g) Niçoise olives

½ cup pickled radishes (page 44)

I love bonito, which is a smaller variety of tuna that is caught along the Basque Country's Atlantic coastline. When I travel to visit my family every summer, I visit the Zallo cannery in the fishing village of Bermeo and buy boxes at wholesale prices. I normally bring back somewhere around sixty cans at a time, which will last me a few months.

In this salad, I take elements of a classic *salade Niçoise* and the *ensalada mixta* I grew up with and add my own twist with fried capers and dill. My mother's version always has soft-cooked carrots in it, and her vinaigrette is made from lemon juice, making it a bit milder than mine. This salad makes for a quick and hearty dinner and lends itself to feeding large crowds when you need to scale up.

MAKES 4 TO 6 SERVINGS

1 Fill a large pot with water and bring to a boil over high heat. Fill a large bowl with ice water. Gently lower the eggs into the boiling water, making sure they don't crack, and add the potatoes. Set a timer for 8 minutes. Remove the eggs from the boiling water and immediately submerge in the ice water. Add the haricots verts to the boiling water and cook for 2 minutes. By then, the potatoes should also be cooked through. Check them by inserting the tip of a knife into the center—it should slide in easily. Continue cooking for a couple more minutes if the potatoes are not done. Drain the potatoes and beans in a colander and submerge in ice water until cool, about 3 minutes.

2 Peel and halve the eggs, then arrange on a large platter. Heat 2 tablespoons of the olive oil in a small sauté pan over medium-high heat. Add the capers, carefully as they might splatter, and cook for 1 minute, then spoon over the eggs.

3 In a small bowl, whisk together the remaining 3 tablespoons olive oil, vinegar, mustard, dill, and salt. Toss the potatoes with 2 tablespoons of the vinaigrette and pile beside the eggs.

4 On a platter, build the salad with piles of the greens, haricots verts, tuna, tomatoes, avocados, olives, and pickled radishes and drizzle everything with the remaining vinaigrette. Garnish with more dill sprigs if desired. It can be served as a composed salad or you can toss it all together.

Tortilla de Patatas with Romaine, Fennel, and Green Olive Salad

Whenever someone that has visited Spain learns where I am from, their first question is always: "Can you teach me how to make *tortilla de patatas*?" Tortilla de patatas is what mothers make for children when they go on field trips, what's prepared for a casual dinner or a birthday party. It's what we eat for elevenses with a cortado or a beer. Any time of day, really. I often make the comparison that tortilla is for Spaniards what hot dogs are for New Yorkers. But certainly way better for you.

One thing to note: you must use a nonstick skillet. The recipe won't work with a cast-iron or stainless steel pan. Invest in a good nontoxic nonstick pan. Also, don't be intimidated by the amount of olive oil. Most of it gets strained out at the end.

MAKES 4 SERVINGS

For the tortilla de patatas
¾ cup (170 g) extra-virgin olive oil
½ medium yellow onion, cut into ¼-inch dice
3 medium (1½ pounds or 680 g) Yukon Gold potatoes, peeled and cut into ½-inch dice
1½ teaspoons kosher salt, divided
6 large eggs

1 To make the tortilla, heat the olive oil in a 10-inch nonstick sauté pan over medium heat. Add the onion and cook for 1 to 2 minutes, or until translucent but not browned.

2 Add the diced potatoes and 1 teaspoon of the salt. Keep the heat on medium for about 2 minutes, then lower it to medium low for about 15 minutes. You aren't really frying the potatoes but poaching them in olive oil. Keep the heat low so the oil simmers very gently. If the potatoes are not falling apart after 15 minutes, I take a fork and gently mash them a bit so the olive oil gets inside them as well. The potatoes should be tender and golden with some pieces caramelized.

3 While the potatoes are cooking, whisk the eggs and the remaining ½ teaspoon salt in a medium bowl. Using a spider or slotted spoon, lift the potatoes out of the pan and into the eggs, draining off as much oil as possible. The potatoes might scramble a bit of the eggs, but this is OK. Stir the eggs and potatoes together.

For the salad

2 small heads baby romaine
  (Little Gem), or 1 large head
  romaine, leaves washed but
  left whole
1 small bulb fennel, thinly shaved
½ cup whole Castelvetrano olives
  or other variety of choice
1 orange, zested and juiced
2 tablespoons extra-virgin
  olive oil
1 tablespoon red wine vinegar
1 teaspoon Dijon mustard
½ teaspoon flaky sea salt
½ teaspoon freshly ground
  black pepper

4   Pour most of the olive oil into a bowl, leaving about 1 tablespoon in the pan. Return the pan to the stove over medium-high heat. Add the potato mixture, and with a wooden spoon, stir the center so the eggs start to cook. When they begin to scramble, stop stirring. Tuck in the edges nicely with a spatula and cook for about 2 minutes.

5   Place a large plate facedown over the pan. Hold the plate tightly with one hand and the pan handle tightly with the other (use a towel if the handle is hot). Flip the tortilla onto the plate. Slide the tortilla back into the sauté pan and cook the other side for 2 to 3 minutes, or until golden brown. I personally like when the center of the tortilla is a bit soft and runny, but cook it as thoroughly as you prefer.

6   Slide the cooked tortilla onto a clean plate, and let it sit for 10 minutes before cutting.

7   While the tortilla is cooling, make the salad. Arrange the romaine, fennel, and olives on a platter. In a small bowl, whisk together the orange juice and zest, olive oil, vinegar, Dijon mustard, salt, and pepper. Drizzle the dressing over the salad.

8   Slice the tortilla into wedges and serve with the salad while warm.

Crispy Chickpeas with Rice, Sweet Potatoes, Avocados, and Greens

1 (15-ounce or 425-g) can
   chickpeas, rinsed and drained
6 tablespoons extra-virgin olive
   oil, divided
2½ teaspoons flaky sea salt,
   divided
2 medium (1½ pounds or 700 g)
   sweet potatoes, peeled and
   cut into 1-inch dice
1 bunch (10 ounces or 280 g)
   broccolini, trimmed and larger
   pieces halved lengthwise
1 teaspoon dried thyme leaves
1 teaspoon ground cumin
1 teaspoon paprika
½ teaspoon freshly ground
   black pepper
1 cup (200 g) brown rice
2 cups (450 g) cold water
1 tablespoon apple cider vinegar
2 teaspoons maple syrup
1 teaspoon Dijon mustard
2 cups peppery greens, such as
   arugula, mizuna, or watercress
2 avocados, peeled, pitted, and
   quartered

This is a large vegetable and legume bowl that has all the textures and the ideal balance of sweetness, acidity, and a touch of spice. I make this regularly on meatless weekday nights. All the components are seasoned separately and take approximately the same time to cook, so while the rice is on the stove, the chickpeas and vegetables are roasting in the oven. It is all bound by a tangy maple-mustard vinaigrette.

MAKES 4 SERVINGS

1 Preheat the oven to 375 degrees F.

2 Pat dry the chickpeas and toss with 1 tablespoon of the olive oil and 1 teaspoon of the salt on a baking sheet. On another baking sheet, toss together the sweet potatoes and broccolini with 3 tablespoons of the olive oil, 1 teaspoon of the salt, and the thyme, cumin, paprika, and pepper. Place both baking sheets in the oven, on separate racks, and bake until the chickpeas are crispy and the sweet potatoes and broccolini are tender and begin to caramelize, 30 to 35 minutes.

3 Meanwhile, combine the rice, water, and remaining ½ teaspoon salt in a medium saucepan. Cover and bring to a simmer over medium-high heat. When the first signs of steam and bubbles appear, reduce the heat to low and cook, covered, until the rice is tender, about 30 minutes. Remove from the heat and keep covered until ready to serve.

4 When the chickpeas and sweet potatoes are done, let them cool for 5 minutes. Fluff the rice with a fork.

5 In a medium bowl, whisk together the remaining 2 tablespoons olive oil, vinegar, maple syrup, and mustard. Add the greens and toss to coat.

6 In a large serving bowl, mix together the chickpeas and rice. Top with the sweet potatoes, broccolini, avocados, and greens. Serve immediately.

Squash, Leek, and Potato Soup with Cheese Toast

This soup is another Basque classic called *porrusalda*, which translates to something like "leek broth." In the original Basque recipe, pieces of carrot, squash, leek, and potato float in a brothy soup. However, I have always preferred it blended because it yields a creamy, silky version instead. And this is why my children started referring to it as "orange soup."

MAKES 6 SERVINGS

3 tablespoons extra-virgin olive oil, divided

1 medium leek (white and light-green parts only), thinly sliced

½ medium yellow onion, diced

2 cloves garlic, minced

1 small (2 pounds or 1 kg) butternut squash, peeled, seeded, and cut into ½-inch dice

2 medium (1 pound or 454 g) Yukon Gold potatoes, peeled and cut into ½-inch dice

1¼ teaspoons kosher salt, divided

3 cups (675 g) chicken stock (page 53) or vegetable stock (page 56), plus more if needed

6 thick slices Sourdough Boules (page 103), toasted

6 ounces (170 g) gruyère cheese, coarsely grated

2 cups peppery greens, such as arugula, mizuna, or watercress

¼ cup raw pepitas (pumpkin seeds), for garnish

1   Heat 2 tablespoons of the olive oil in a Dutch oven over medium-high heat. Add the leek, onion, and garlic. Stir and cook for 3 minutes, or until tender. Add the squash, potatoes, and 1 teaspoon of the salt. Stir and cook for 5 minutes. Add the stock, cover, and simmer for 20 minutes, or until all the vegetables are tender.

2   Preheat the broiler.

3   Transfer the soup to a high-speed blender on medium for about 1 minute or until smooth. Be careful as hot liquids expand, so you may need to process in batches. Alternatively, use an immersion blender to puree the soup in the pot. Taste and adjust the seasoning if needed. Add more stock if you prefer a thinner consistency. The soup can be made 3 days in advance—in fact, I like it best the next day. It thickens in the refrigerator, but you can loosen it with a bit more stock when reheating.

4   Arrange the bread slices on a baking sheet and sprinkle with the cheese. Broil for about 1 minute, or until the cheese has melted and starts to brown.

5   Toss together the greens with the remaining 1 tablespoon olive oil and ¼ teaspoon salt. Serve the soup in bowls and sprinkle with some pepitas. Top the cheese toast with the greens and serve on the side.

Roasted Cauliflower, Swiss Chard, and Hazelnut Pasta

There is a lot going on in this pasta dish: the smokiness from the roasted cauliflower, the earthy cumin, the briny anchovies, the tender chard, the crunch from the hazelnuts. If you are avoiding grains, you can make this without the pasta and instead serve it with a fried egg and some fresh herbs. This makes for a great lunch too.

MAKES 4 TO 6 SERVINGS

1 small (1½ pounds or 680 g) head cauliflower, cut into medium florets

5 tablespoons extra-virgin olive oil, divided

2 teaspoons ground cumin

2 thyme sprigs

1½ teaspoons kosher salt, divided

½ teaspoon freshly ground black pepper, divided

12 ounces (340 g) gluten-free dry spaghetti or fresh pasta (page 228)

2 oil-packed anchovy fillets (optional)

2 cloves garlic, thinly sliced

4 packed cups chopped Swiss chard (about 5 leaves and stems)

1 lemon, zested and juiced

2 tablespoons finely chopped Italian parsley

2 tablespoons coarsely chopped toasted hazelnuts

2 tablespoons finely grated Parmesan cheese

1   Preheat the oven to 400 degrees F. Toss together the cauliflower, 3 tablespoons of the olive oil, cumin, thyme, 1 teaspoon of the salt, and pepper on a baking sheet, making sure the cauliflower is well coated with oil and spices. Bake for 30 minutes, or until the cauliflower is tender and caramelized.

2   While the cauliflower is baking, fill a large pot with generously salted water and bring it to a boil. Add the spaghetti, stir, and cook until al dente, about 10 minutes (check box for cooking time if not using fresh pasta). Reserve ½ cup of the pasta cooking water before draining.

3   Heat the remaining 2 tablespoons olive oil in a large sauté pan over medium heat. Add the anchovies and garlic. Stir and cook for 30 seconds, until the anchovies dissolve into the oil, then add the Swiss chard and remaining ½ teaspoon salt. Toss together and cook for 3 minutes, or until the chard is wilted. Add the reserved pasta water and simmer for 5 minutes.

4   Increase heat to medium high. Add the spaghetti, roasted cauliflower, and lemon juice and zest to the pan, and toss everything together for about 1 minute. Serve immediately with a sprinkle of parsley, hazelnuts, and Parmesan.

Lentil and Root Vegetable Stew with Broccoli Rabe and Fried Eggs

When I think of the dishes my mother made for our family growing up, lentil stew comes to mind first and foremost. Apparently I wasn't particularly fond of it at the time. I do remember my mother sitting next to me at the kitchen table well after everyone else had finished their bowls of stew, still trying to feed me a few spoonfuls of the warm, meaty broth. Today it's hard to imagine how I could have disliked this dish because it is one of my favorite comfort foods. I make it at least once a week during the colder months, and my children often take it to school for lunch the next day.

MAKES 6 SERVINGS

1 cup French lentils or other lentils of choice

5 tablespoons extra-virgin olive oil, divided

1 medium onion, cut into ¼-inch dice

2 medium carrots, peeled and cut into ¼-inch dice

1 stalk celery, cut into ¼-inch dice

1 clove garlic, minced

1¾ teaspoons kosher salt, divided

½ teaspoon freshly ground black pepper

6 ounces (170 g) Spanish cured chorizo, cut into ¼-inch slices

1 medium sweet potato, peeled and cut into ¼-inch dice

1 medium Yukon Gold potato, peeled and cut into ¼-inch dice

1 medium turnip, peeled and cut into ¼-inch dice

1 tablespoon tomato paste

1 quart (1 liter) chicken stock (page 53)

5 sprigs thyme

8 ounces (225 g) broccoli rabe or other bitter green, ends trimmed

6 large eggs

1 Rinse the lentils in a fine-mesh sieve under cold running water until the water runs clear. Shake them around and remove any debris you find.

2 Heat 3 tablespoons of the olive oil in a 7-quart Dutch oven over medium-high heat. Add the onion, carrots, celery, garlic, ½ teaspoon of the salt, and pepper. Stir and cook for about 5 minutes, or until the vegetables are tender. Stir in the chorizo, potatoes, turnip, and tomato paste and cook for 2 minutes. Add the chicken stock, lentils, thyme, and 1 teaspoon salt. Stir, cover, and bring the liquid to a simmer over medium-high heat. Reduce the heat to medium low and cook for 35 to 40 minutes, or until the lentils are tender. Taste and adjust the seasoning. Add a bit of stock or water if the stew seems too dry. Pick out the thyme sprigs and discard.

3 Meanwhile, heat 1 tablespoon olive oil in a medium sauté pan over medium heat. Add the broccoli rabe, remaining salt, and cook for 5 minutes, giving the pan several good shakes. Set aside.

4 Heat a medium cast-iron or nonstick sauté pan over medium-high heat. Add the remaining 1 tablespoon of olive oil and crack in two eggs. Cook the eggs until the whites become slightly crispy and the yolks are still runny, about 2 minutes. Alternatively, if you prefer your eggs over easy, you may flip the egg and finish cooking for another 30 seconds. Repeat with remaining four eggs.

5 Divide the lentil stew among bowls. Top with broccoli rabe, an egg, and finish with a crack of black pepper. Serve immediately.

Spaghetti and Meatballs

There are a few recipes in my repertoire that come around when I am about to leave home for a few days on a work trip. I make a large Dutch oven full of spaghetti and meatballs that my children can eat for a few days—even take in their lunch boxes—and likely another large pot of Lentil and Root Vegetable Stew (page 195).

MAKES 4 SERVINGS WITH LEFTOVERS

2 pounds (1 kg) ground beef (or use half ground pork if desired)

2 large eggs, lightly beaten

¼ cup (40 g) gluten-free bread crumbs (see Note)

1 tablespoon finely chopped Italian parsley

3 teaspoons kosher salt, divided

1 teaspoon freshly ground black pepper

4 tablespoons extra-virgin olive oil, divided

1 medium yellow onion, cut into ¼-inch dice

½ medium red bell pepper, cut into ¼-inch dice

3 cloves garlic, minced

1 (28-ounce or 795-g) can tomato puree

2 teaspoons sugar

6 ounces gluten-free dry spaghetti or fresh pasta (page 228)

2 ounces (55 g) finely grated Parmesan cheese

Note: To make homemade bread crumbs, preheat the oven to 250 degrees F. Slice a loaf of gluten-free bread into 2-inch pieces. Place them on a baking sheet and bake for 15 to 20 minutes, or until the bread is completely dried out. Process the bread in a food processor until you have coarse bread crumbs, or longer if you like a finer texture.

1   In a large bowl, combine the beef, eggs, bread crumbs, parsley, 1½ teaspoons of the salt, and black pepper. Using clean hands or gloves, mix the ingredients together until well incorporated, but be careful not to overwork the meat or the meatballs could become a bit tough when cooked. Form the mixture into 1-inch balls, and place them on a tray or baking sheet.

2   Heat 1 tablespoon of the olive oil in a large Dutch oven with a lid over medium-high heat. Add the meatballs and cook until browned on all sides, about 5 minutes. They will finish cooking in the sauce, so it doesn't matter if they are still pink inside. Remove the meatballs and return to the tray.

3   Add the remaining 3 tablespoons olive oil to the same pot. Reduce the heat to medium low and add the onion, bell pepper, garlic, and remaining 1½ teaspoons salt. Stir with a wooden spoon to loosen any brown bits and cook until the vegetables are tender, about 7 minutes. Add the tomato puree and sugar. Stir, reduce the heat to low, and let the sauce simmer for 15 minutes.

4   While the sauce is cooking, fill a large stockpot with generously salted water and bring to a boil over high heat.

5   Transfer the sauce to a blender or food processor and puree until smooth. If it seems too thick, add a bit of beef stock or water. Return the meatballs to the pot, pour the sauce over them, and give the pan a good shake to distribute the sauce. Cover and simmer over low heat for 20 minutes, or until the meatballs are cooked through.

6   Meanwhile, add the spaghetti to the boiling water, stir, and cook until al dente, about 10 minutes. Strain the spaghetti, and add it to the simmering sauce and meatballs. Toss and serve immediately topped with Parmesan.

Crispy Snapper with Root Veggie Mash

This recipe has an unexpected touch: the vanilla seeds added to the parsnip and celery root mash. I cannot recall the first time I tasted vanilla and celery root together, but I remember it blew my mind, and since then I've been wanting to create a recipe that incorporates the two together. And of course, crispy fish skin. My love.

MAKES 4 SERVINGS

For the salsa verde
½ cup (115 g) extra-virgin olive oil
⅓ cup finely chopped Italian
  parsley
⅓ cup finely chopped cilantro
1 clove garlic, finely minced
1 tablespoon freshly squeezed
  lemon juice
½ teaspoon flaky sea salt
¼ teaspoon red pepper flakes

For the parsnip and celery root mash
2 medium parsnips, peeled and
  cut into ½-inch dice
1 medium celery root, peeled
  and cut into ½-inch dice
¾ cup (170 g) whole-milk Greek-
  style yogurt
½ cup (115 g) vegetable stock
  (page 56)
¾ teaspoon flaky sea salt
½ vanilla bean, split lengthwise
  and seeds scraped (optional)

For the crispy snapper
4 (6-ounce) skin-on snapper or
  rockfish fillets
½ teaspoon flaky sea salt
½ teaspoon freshly ground
  black pepper
2 tablespoons extra-virgin olive oil

1   First, make the salsa verde. Whisk together the olive oil, parsley, cilantro, garlic, lemon juice, salt, and red pepper flakes in a small bowl and set aside. The salsa verde will keep for 3 days in the refrigerator.

2   To make the mash, fill a medium saucepan with water and bring it to a boil over high heat. Add the parsnips and celery root and cook until tender, about 15 minutes. Drain into a colander and return to the saucepan. Add the yogurt, stock, salt, and vanilla seeds and mash with a potato masher. You could also puree everything in a food processor if you prefer a smoother texture. Set aside.

3   Finally, prepare the snapper. Pat dry the fish with paper towels and season with the salt and pepper. Heat the olive oil in a large sauté pan over medium-high heat. Add the fillets skin side down and cook for 3 to 4 minutes, until the skin is crispy, then flip and finish cooking for another minute.

4   To serve, spoon some of the parsnip and celery root mash into the center of a plate, place a fillet over it, and top with salsa verde. Serve immediately.

Spicy Lamb Sausage with Yogurt, Herbs, and Fried Egg

This dish can serve equally as a quick everyday supper as it can a hearty weekend brunch—I suppose it's my version of breakfast for dinner. There's nothing complicated about these lamb sausages, but the spices are really important: cumin, coriander, fennel, and Aleppo pepper, which, alongside piment d'Espelette, I am obsessed with. In fact, they are both quite similar. A little smoky, a little spicy. Aleppo comes in a coarser grind than Espelette pepper. You can substitute with half smoked paprika, half cayenne in a pinch.

MAKES 4 SERVINGS

1 teaspoon cumin seeds

½ teaspoon coriander seeds

½ teaspoon fennel seeds

1 pound (454 g) ground lamb

2 cloves garlic, finely minced

2 tablespoons finely chopped Italian parsley, plus more for garnish

2 tablespoons finely chopped cilantro, plus more for garnish

4 teaspoons Aleppo pepper, divided

1¼ teaspoons kosher salt, divided

3 tablespoons extra-virgin olive oil, divided

½ cup (115 g) labneh (page 37) or whole-milk Greek-style yogurt

1 teaspoon freshly grated lemon zest

4 large eggs

2 cups tender greens, such as watercress, baby kale, or spinach

¼ cup dukkah (page 40)

1   Combine the cumin, coriander, and fennel seeds in a small sauté pan over medium heat and toast until fragrant, about 3 minutes. Transfer to a mortar and pestle and crush into a powder. You can also do this in a spice grinder.

2   In a medium bowl, mix together the ground spices, lamb, garlic, parsley, cilantro, 2 teaspoons of the Aleppo pepper, and 1 teaspoon of the salt. Form 8 equal patties approximately 3 inches in diameter, and place them on a large plate. Heat a large sauté pan over medium-high heat. Add 1 tablespoon of olive oil, and cook the sausages for 3 minutes on each side, or until golden brown.

3   Meanwhile, whisk together the labneh, 1 tablespoon of olive oil, lemon zest, and remaining 2 teaspoons Aleppo and ¼ teaspoon salt. Spread the mixture into the centers of four plates. Top with 2 hot sausages each.

4   If the sauté pan used to cook the sausage is too sticky, scrape some of the brown bits. Return the pan to medium-high heat. Add 1 tablespoon of olive oil, and crack two eggs at a time into the pan. Season with a pinch of salt and cook until the whites are crispy and yolks are still runny (flip the egg if you like a firmer yolk). Carefully lift the fried egg from the pan and place on top of the sausage. Top with the greens and dukkah, and serve immediately.

Braised Chicken with Apples and Cider

6 skin-on chicken legs or thighs (about 2 pounds or 1 kg) (see Note)

1½ teaspoons kosher salt

1 teaspoon freshly ground black pepper

2 tablespoons extra-virgin olive oil

1 medium leek (white and light-green parts only), thinly sliced

1 medium shallot, thinly sliced

6 cloves garlic, peeled and crushed

3 sprigs thyme

1 cup (225 g) Basque-style cider

1 large sprig tarragon

4 whole small apples, or 2 large ones, quartered and cored

2 tablespoons finely chopped Italian parsley

Note: If you prefer, use split bone-in chicken breast and cut in half. Cook as directed.

Most Basque people love cider, and I am one of them. Cider has as much historical and cultural meaning in the Basque Country as it does gastronomical. It is said to have been the cure for scurvy for the fishermen and explorers that survived in the sea for months at a time. Naturally fermenting apples is a centuries-old tradition—there is no filtering, and the process simply relies on the native yeast that already exists on the skin of the apple. The result is cider that is very dry, funky, puckering, and murky, which is very different from the filtered sweet ciders found in the US. This recipe is one I grew up with, and I go back to it when I need some comfort food.

My grandmother Miren used to make this at the pastry shop kitchen to feed large family gatherings. She used the Reinette variety of apples—sweet and firm but with a very distinct flavor that is hard to describe—which she also used to make all the apple tarts that were sold in the pastry shop. I loved finishing all the remaining pan sauce with a large chunk of bread.

If you cannot find Basque-style cider, you can use half hard cider, half apple cider vinegar. Serve the chicken with a simple green salad.

MAKES 6 SERVINGS

1 Pat dry the chicken with paper towels, then season it on all sides with the salt and pepper. Heat the olive oil in a large cast-iron pan with a lid over medium-high heat. Add the chicken and cook until golden brown on all sides, about 6 minutes per side. Remove the chicken to a plate.

2 Reduce the heat to medium and add the leek, shallot, garlic, and thyme to the pan. Stir and scrape up any brown bits and cook until the vegetables are tender, about 5 minutes. Add the cider and tarragon, stir, and return the chicken to the pan. Nestle the apples all around, cover, and cook over medium heat for 25 minutes, or until the chicken reaches 165 degrees F. Uncover, increase the heat to high, and reduce the liquid until the apples begin to caramelize, 3 to 5 minutes. Sprinkle with the parsley and serve immediately.

Slow-Roasted Salmon with Fennel, Citrus, and Harissa

½ cup (115 g) extra-virgin olive oil

¼ cup spicy harissa or chili paste

2 cloves garlic, thinly sliced

2 small lemons, thinly sliced

1 small bulb fennel, thinly sliced (reserve some fronds for garnish)

½ medium onion, thinly sliced

1 (2-pound or 1-kg) skinless salmon fillet, preferably wild

1½ teaspoons flaky sea salt

1 teaspoon freshly ground black pepper

¼ cup tender herbs, such as parsley, dill, and chives

This is one of my favorite ways to cook salmon—cooking it at a low temperature helps retain so much of its tenderness and moisture. My children love it over a pile of rice with a simple green salad. I often save the leftovers to toss into a salad the next day with bitter greens, avocado, and green olives.

MAKES 6 SERVINGS

1   Preheat the oven to 275 degrees F. In a small bowl, whisk together the olive oil, harissa, and garlic. Spread half of the mixture on the bottom of a 12-inch cast-iron pan. Add the lemon, fennel, and onion to the pan and toss together to coat with the harissa olive oil mixture. Season the salmon with salt and pepper on both sides. Place on top of the vegetables and pour the remaining harissa olive oil over the top, making sure it coats the fish.

2   Bake the salmon for 20 minutes. Baste the top with some of the oil from the pan, and bake for another 15 to 20 minutes, or until the salmon is tender with a tinge of pink in the center. Transfer the salmon to a platter.

3   Set the pan on the stovetop, and cook the vegetables over high heat until they begin to caramelize, about 3 minutes. Flake the salmon with a fork and top with the caramelized vegetables and tender herbs.

CHAPTER SIX

The
Gathering
Table

Cooking is a means of communication for me, and sharing a meal is an opportunity to make connections with others. Inviting people into my home supplies the sense of community I felt growing up. Even as a small girl, I was always included at the table. The notion of a "kids'" table is not one I am familiar with, and I love the intergenerational component of including my children in these gatherings. Whether it's the awe in their eyes as friends carry on or the small token of wisdom they offer at the most unexpected times, nothing gives me more pleasure than seeing a table full of friends and family passing platters of food, pouring drinks, enjoying heady talks about philosophy, or even arguing over politics. The gathering table should be a safe space where we show vulnerability that will forever bond those around it. These big dishes are meant to open you up to inviting others in, creating a medium for the rich conversation that nourishes our souls.

This chapter is divided into small menus that are inspired by mood and season. The recipes require a little more preparation time, and so many of the components can be made in advance and put together right before serving. Handmade pasta can be rolled and cut in the morning with a pot of slow-braised ragù on the stove, coming together in a few short minutes after the pasta is finally dropped in the boiling water and then tossed into the sauce. There is also outdoor cooking, which is the best way to spend summer nights—paella over an open fire and grilled pizzas in the backyard. Winter evenings are for buttermilk-brined roasted chicken or my mom's hearty fish soup with aioli and gruyère tartines.

A SPANISH GATHERING

MENU

Chicken and Seafood Paella on an Open Fire

Grilled Green Tomato and Eggplant Salad

Peach Txakoli Cocktail

There are a lot of mixed emotions that come with being a longtime expat. How things were and how they have evolved without you there as witness. Feeling divided and lacking a true sense of place with one foot here and one foot there. Cooking for other people is often an expression of this feeling. It's revealing and intimate—a conversation piece that always leads me back to family. Because even if buildings have gone up or fashions change, my friends and family back home are still cooking the same recipes we cooked decades ago. Making these dishes connects me with that "here and there" and grounds me in the in-between.

There is no more iconic Spanish recipe than paella. Disclaimer here: I am not from Valencia, which is where paella originated. Paella is practically a religion in Valencia, and anything that steers from tradition is considered sacrilege. Authentic Valencian paella doesn't have chorizo, and some say seafood and other meats should not be mixed. This version is the one I grew up with, and to all those purists, my apologies. What we all agree on, however, is the importance of the *socarrat*—the rice sticking to the bottom of the pan that becomes dark and crispy. A paella should always have the socarrat, and everyone I know fights for it. For this, the most important thing is that after the liquid is added to the rice, you give everything in the pan one good stir, then never stir it again.

A note about the rice: I will say that even in Seattle, with its many specialty markets, I search for bomba rice, which is the short-grain rice grown in Valencia and that paella is made with. If you cannot find bomba, go for arborio, and it will work well.

Chicken and Seafood Paella on an Open Fire

Although you can certainly cook paella indoors, there really is something special about cooking outdoors. Invest in a paella pan; this recipe calls for a 15-inch one. It is important to use a pan that is shallow and wide. The shape ensures that the rice cooks evenly in one layer—and more socarrat for all.

Try to find prawns with the head on because they give so much flavor to the paella. Use shell-on shrimp as an alternative. Finally, a note about clams: Keep them stored in the refrigerator until you are ready to use. Discard any broken ones and do not eat any clams that remain closed after cooking.

MAKES 6 TO 8 SERVINGS

1 quart (1 liter) chicken stock (page 53)

4 threads saffron

1 pound (454 g) skin-on boneless chicken thighs, cut into 2-inch pieces

1 teaspoon kosher salt

1 teaspoon freshly ground black pepper

3 tablespoons extra-virgin olive oil

1 medium yellow onion, cut into ¼-inch pieces

2 cloves garlic, minced

2 very ripe tomatoes, cut into ¼-inch dice

8 ounces green beans, ends trimmed and cut into 1-inch pieces

6 ounces cured chorizo, sliced ¼ inch thick

2 cups (400 g) bomba or arborio rice

1½ pounds (680 g) prawns or shrimp, preferably with the heads on

1 pound (454 g) clams, rinsed in cold water

1 pound (454 g) mussels, rinsed in cold water and beards removed

1 lemon, thinly sliced

2 tablespoons finely chopped Italian parsley

1 Make a wood fire or light charcoals. Place a metal grid on top big enough to fit the paella pan and a saucepan. Pour the stock into the saucepan, and add the saffron threads. Keep in an area where there is no direct heat so the stock is just warmed. Do not let it boil.

2 Place the paella pan in the center of the hottest area. You might have to move it around as the fire progresses and varies. Season the chicken with the salt and pepper. Add the olive oil to the pan, and cook the chicken until caramelized on all sides, about 5 minutes. Transfer the chicken to a plate and set aside.

3 Add the onion and garlic, stir, and cook until translucent, about 3 minutes. Add the tomatoes, stir, and cook for 2 minutes. Return the chicken to the pan, add the greens beans and chorizo, and cook for 1 minute. Add the rice and stir for 1 minute, until it is well coated with the oil and well incorporated. Pour in the warm stock and stir once. This is the only time you should stir the paella. Now it will cook over the fire, uncovered, for 18 minutes. Make sure the stock simmers nicely but not so aggressively that it evaporates quickly. Move the paella pan around to keep the heat as consistent as possible.

4 Add the prawns, clams, and mussels. Tightly cover the pan with aluminum foil and continue cooking for another 5 to 7 minutes, until the clams and mussels open and the shrimp is pink. Remove the pan from the fire, keep it covered, and let it rest for 5 minutes. Remove the foil, arrange the lemon slices on top, sprinkle with the parsley, and serve immediately.

How to Build a Fire

Building a good fire is as important as any of the ingredients in this paella recipe. The beautiful thing about cooking paella over an open fire is that the heat of the fire will reach all sides of the pan, cooking it evenly, unlike a gas stove, which is unlikely to have a wide enough burner.

First, find a safe place to build the fire away from trees and bushes. Use a fire pit with a grill grate on top, or if you are going to build one, dig a small hole in the ground or sand and surround it with rocks.

Stack twigs and small branches, then light them with matches. As the fire builds, you can add dry wood logs (any wood works). Add more logs as needed to give yourself plenty of hot coals to work with. Place a large grill grate 6 to 8 inches above the fire, making sure it is as level as possible and large enough that you can move the pan around in case you need different heat levels during cooking. As the logs burn down and are glowing red with embers, use long tongs to move them under the grate. When you can hold your hand over the grate for just a few seconds before it's too hot, it's time to start cooking. Keep moving coals under the grate as needed while cooking, or add a couple new logs if you need some more heat. Move the paella pan to different spots on the grate so the liquid doesn't evaporate too rapidly and to maintain a steady simmer.

A friendly reminder: never leave a fire unattended—be sure to put it out when you're done.

Grilled Green Tomato and Eggplant Salad

At summer's end when my tomato plants are left with unripe fruit, I go to this salad. You could also make it with fresh ripe tomatoes, but there would be no need to grill them then. There is something about the acidic green tomatoes that works so well when cooked.

Also, I like to use the thinner and smaller Japanese eggplants for this salad and grill them whole, but larger ones will work. If your eggplant is large, you might want to slice it in half lengthwise and grill it that way.

MAKES 6 SERVINGS

1 pound (454 g) unripe green tomatoes, sliced ½ inch thick

1 pound (454 g) eggplant

4 tablespoons extra-virgin olive oil, divided

1½ teaspoons flaky sea salt

1 teaspoon ground cumin

1 teaspoon ground coriander

1 lime, zested and juiced

1 tablespoon sherry or red wine vinegar

¼ medium red onion, thinly sliced

½ small serrano pepper, seeded and minced

⅓ cup almonds, toasted and coarsely chopped

1 Heat a grill or griddle over medium-high heat. Brush the tomato slices and eggplant with 2 tablespoons of the olive oil, then sprinkle the salt, cumin, and coriander all over. Grill the tomatoes until tender, about 5 minutes on each side. Grill the eggplant until the skin is blistered and the flesh is tender, about 7 minutes on each side.

2 Transfer the tomatoes and eggplant to a large platter. Drizzle with the lime juice and zest and vinegar. Top with the onion, serrano, and almonds, then drizzle with the remaining 2 tablespoons olive oil. Serve immediately.

Peach Txakoli Cocktail

2 ripe medium peaches, thinly
  sliced
2 cups (450 g) *txakoli* or other
  dry young white wine
1 cup (225 g) peach shrub
  (page 47)

I was inspired to create a recipe that is a twist on classic
sangria—though, like my paella, I am afraid the orthodox
sangria lovers might consider this sacrilege, so I don't dare
call it sangria. In the Basque Country, we like acid and our
profile definitely leans toward the less sweet. *Txakoli* is a
young, acidic white wine from the Basque Country, which
is now available in most wine shops and even supermarkets
across the US. It can easily be substituted by Portuguese
Vinho Verde or another dry white you love, but definitely
use one that is dry and slightly acidic.

MAKES 6 SERVINGS

1   Mix together all the ingredients in a pitcher, chill for at least
1 hour, and serve over ice.

Setting a Mood

I love to set a simple table, one with mismatched plates, and vintage flatware and glasses. I shy away from overly styled tables that can feel cluttered or formal. I want my guests to feel like they can use every single thing that is in front of them. I lean toward very neutral tones so the colors won't distract too much from the food. I think about what we will be eating and put out only what pieces are necessary to enjoy it, keeping things as unfussy as possible. Often, this might be just a dinner plate, fork, and knife, or maybe a bowl and spoon if I'm serving soup. I never bother with side plates or extra flatware.

Flatware

When I was in my late teens and still living with my parents, my mom was given a flatware set when she opened an account at a local bank. I know it sounds bizarre in today's world, but that's how it was back then—flatware, vacuum cleaners, knives . . . the bank gave customers such items. I still clearly remember arriving home from school and my mother showing me the large box full of stainless steel flatware. For you, she said. At the time I thought I would never have use for such a thing. It seemed outdated, and I couldn't envision a life where I would actually need a set of forks. But today, that flatware is still my everyday set, and any attempts I have made to retire them have backfired when my children complain. They love them (and I secretly do too).

The rest of my flatware is vintage, bought mostly at consignment shops, thrift stores, or flea markets. Something about old flatware adds a touch of comfort and ease to a table. I love a spoon with a pronounced tip and forks with weight and sharp edges. Vintage knives with a dullish blade are OK for certain things—maybe vegetables, fish, or spreading butter, but if meat is served, make sure you provide appropriate knives for your guests.

Linens

My studio kitchen drawers are filled with linens organized by color tone. They give me enormous pleasure, but I am not too precious about them either, because I love the patina linens get from being used and washed and used and washed over and over again. I hardly ever buy proper tablecloths—instead I buy large pieces of washed soft linen from my friend Keli's fabric shop and use them on my table, even with raw hems. And I collect linens from my travels just like I do ceramics.

Another inexpensive option I love is the basic white IKEA Tekla kitchen linens that cost about a dollar each. Years ago, *Martha Stewart Living* magazine showed how to dye these kitchen towels in various neutral tones, and that was the greatest idea ever. So for one of the first dinners I hosted in my studio when I moved to Seattle, I bought basic white napkins, and my friend Jenn Elliott-Blake, one of my favorite stylists, dyed them in different tones of grayish blue. These are still some of my favorite and most used napkins. Another trick Jenn taught me: never iron linens. They feel more inviting when they are a bit unruly and rumpled.

Lastly, don't forget about impromptu picnics. Carry some linen fabric or a quilt or a wool blanket in your car in case you want to gather some portable food and create a beautiful outdoor picnic.

Flowers

Just like everything else on the table, I want the flowers to feel very organic, seasonal, and unstyled. I don't want them to interfere with the conversation around the table or become an obstruction, so I keep it simple by scattering glass or ceramic vases around with small bouquets or even a single stem in them.

Perhaps because I am not a floral designer, I prefer small bunches of wildflowers I find around the neighborhood in the summertime, branches of blooming trees in the spring, foliage leaves in the fall, and evergreen pine branches or rosemary in the winter. I have several David Austin rosebushes around my home that bloom from May until November—some are white, some a light pink-coral, others a barely-there yellow. They are hearty on the bush but delicate once cut. They are beautiful, and it brings me so much joy to decorate my dining table with them.

My friend Jenn taught me to hang branches from the ceiling for a dramatic effect and to always carry clippers when I take walks around the neighborhood and city since you never know what you are going to find. She also visits a local wholesale flower market anytime she needs something in abundance, so see if you have access to a flower market or grower near you.

HOMEMADE PASTA DINNER

MENU

Homemade Pasta

Braised Beef Ragù with Tagliatelle

Radicchio, Apple, and Celery Root Salad with Buttermilk–Poppy Seed Vinaigrette

Homemade pasta is a breeze. I get the ragù going, and as soon as the pot is in the oven, I begin making the pasta. It doesn't take much time at all; however, I leave it for those days when the house is quiet and I crave some solitude in the kitchen. I knead, I roll, I shape—all in a very steady, organized manner. To save time, both the pasta and the ragù can be made in advance. It all comes together in an instant. Just before guests are to sit at the table, reheat the ragù and drop the pasta in boiling water. Toss the salad, and set everything out family-style.

Homemade Pasta

1½ cups (210 g) superfine brown
   rice flour, plus more for dusting
½ cup plus 1 tablespoon (90 g)
   potato starch
3 teaspoons xanthan gum
1½ teaspoons kosher salt
3 large whole eggs plus
   6 egg yolks
1½ tablespoons extra-virgin
   olive oil

Making pasta from scratch sounds like a big undertaking, but it's surprisingly simple. For best results, I have a few tips. I know I sound like a broken record when I speak about weighing ingredients, but seriously, it's particularly important in making pasta and having the same smooth texture every time.

Brown rice flour that is not finely milled will work, but the dough won't be as smooth as if you use superfine. It can also result in stickier dough that falls apart easier when rolling and cutting it with a pasta machine. Because the flour particles are larger, they don't hydrolyze as well. Try letting the pasta dough rest an hour or two longer, which should help.

Keep your work area clean. Making pasta can be a bit messy, especially your first couple of tries. For this, a bench scraper is very useful, as it will help you keep your area clean and free of clumpy bits of dough. Wash your hands between kneadings as needed.

This recipe is for a basic egg pasta, but you can flavor it by adding 1 tablespoon of paste, such as squid ink, beet puree, or finely chopped steamed nettles (after squeezing out any excess liquid). If you add a paste, you may need to add a couple teaspoons more of the brown rice flour as well.

MAKES APPROXIMATELY 20 OUNCES (570 G)
PASTA DOUGH, FOR ABOUT 6 SERVINGS

1   In a medium bowl, whisk together the brown rice flour, potato starch, xanthan gum, and salt. Pile the mixture in a mound on a work surface and form a well in the center. (It should resemble something like a volcano.)

2   Add the whole eggs, yolks, and olive oil to the center of the well. Gently whisk the eggs with a fork while using your other hand to hold the walls of flour in place. Move the fork around, whisking to incorporate more and more flour into the eggs. Don't worry if egg oozes out—bring it back into the center and keeping whisking in the flour. It will be messy and look like a lumpy mass. Using a bench scraper, bring the dough together in the center and form it into a ball. I always wash my hands at this point before kneading.

3   Knead the dough together until it feels smooth. This can take up anywhere from 5 to 10 minutes. Try not to pull and knead as you might imagine bread—there is not enough elasticity in the dough to create those long strands, so simply knead by pushing down on the dough, bringing it together, and pushing down again. When the dough feels smooth, wrap it in plastic wrap and let it rest on the counter for 30 minutes. Clean the work surface, and set up a pasta machine.

4   Cut the dough into eight pieces. Work with one piece at a time, keeping the others wrapped in plastic. Roll the dough into a rectangle with a rolling pin so that it fits through the largest setting of the pasta machine. Trim if needed to keep the edges sharp and clean. Roll the dough through the machine three times. Change to a smaller setting and roll three more times. Continue rolling until the sheet is about $\frac{1}{16}$ inch thick (number 5 in my pasta-rolling machine), trimming the edges if needed. Dust the work surface with brown rice flour, and lay the sheet of dough on top. Cover with plastic and repeat with the remaining dough pieces, layering plastic between each sheet.

5   Once all the dough has been rolled, it's time to cut the pasta. Run each sheet of pasta through the tagliatelle cutter setting in your pasta machine, which is a bit wider than $\frac{1}{4}$ inch thick. You can also cut the pasta by hand using a pastry or pizza cutter. Once cut, shape the pasta into nests. The pasta can be frozen on a baking sheet covered with plastic wrap for up to 3 months.

Braised Beef Ragù with Tagliatelle

This is such a classic stew that you can simply make it on its own and serve it with a loaf of bread and green salad, but I love it tossed with fresh pasta. As is true of most stews, ragù is great made a day in advance and then reheated, as the flavors intensify.

MAKES 6 TO 8 SERVINGS

2 pounds (1 kg)
    boneless beef chuck roast, cut
    into 2-inch cubes
1½ teaspoons kosher salt
1 teaspoon freshly ground black
    pepper
1 tablespoon extra-virgin olive
    oil
1 medium red onion, cut into
    ¼-inch dice
1 medium carrot, peeled and cut
    into ¼-inch dice
1 stalk celery, cut into ¼-inch
    dice
5 cloves garlic, minced
2 sprigs thyme
1 sprig rosemary
1 (28-ounce or 795-g) can
    crushed tomatoes
2 cups (450 g) red wine, such as
    pinot noir or cabernet
Fresh tagliatelle pasta (page 228)
3 ounces (90 g) freshly
    grated Parmigiano-Reggiano
3 tablespoons finely chopped
    Italian parsley

1 Preheat the oven to 275 degrees F.

2 Pat dry the beef with paper towels. Season the beef on all sides with the salt and pepper. Heat the olive oil in a large Dutch oven over medium-high heat. Add the beef without crowding the pot too much—cook in two batches if necessary. Let the beef caramelize on all sides, about 7 minutes total, and transfer to a large plate.

3 Add the onion, carrot, celery, garlic, thyme, and rosemary to the pot and stir with a wooden spoon, scraping up any brown bits from the bottom. Cook the vegetables until tender, about 5 minutes. Add the tomatoes and red wine and stir well. Return the beef to the pot and stir.

4 Bring the stew to a simmer, cover the pot, and place it in the oven. Cook, stirring occasionally, for 3 hours, until the meat is falling apart. Pick out the thyme and rosemary sprigs and discard. Shred the beef with a fork or tongs and keep warm on the stove over low heat. If you make the ragù the day before, simply let it cool down to room temperature, then store in the refrigerator. I put the whole pot straight into the fridge. When ready to serve, reheat it over low heat for 15 to 20 minutes, stirring occasionally.

5 Fill a large stockpot with generously salted water and bring to a boil over high heat. Add the tagliatelle and cook for 2 to 3 minutes, or until al dente. Drain in a colander, reserving some of the cooking water to loosen the ragù if it seems too dry.

6 Stir the pasta into the warm sauce so it has a chance to absorb it. Serve immediately topped with the Parmigiano-Reggiano and parsley.

Radicchio, Apple, and Celery Root Salad with Buttermilk–Poppy Seed Vinaigrette

Salad combinations with thinly sliced apple, celery root, and poppy seeds appear in many of my fall and winter meals, adding necessary crunch and sweetness to the often-bitter greens of the colder months. Celery root, the ugly and underrated bulb I have watched dull on many supermarket shelves, is indeed one of my favorite things to cook. Once you cut through the thick and fuzzy exterior, you will find its aromatic white flesh. It is delicious added to vegetable soups, mashed together with potatoes, or raw in salads.

MAKES 6 SERVINGS

1   In a large serving bowl, whisk together the buttermilk, olive oil, poppy seeds, salt, and pepper. Add the radicchio, apple, celery root, and radishes, then toss together with the vinaigrette to coat evenly. Serve immediately.

¼ cup (55 g) full-fat buttermilk
2 tablespoons extra-virgin olive oil
1 tablespoon poppy seeds
1 teaspoon flaky sea salt
½ teaspoon freshly ground
  black pepper
2 medium heads radicchio, core
  removed, quartered, and thinly
  sliced
1 medium apple, cored and
  thinly sliced
1 small bulb celery root, peeled,
  halved, and thinly sliced
  crosswise
4 radishes, thinly sliced

THE GARDEN
AND THE SEA

_____

MENU

My Mom's Fish Soup

Aioli and Gruyère Tartines

*Peppery Greens with
Mustard-Honey Vinaigrette*

I grew up in a valley, surrounded by the western foothills of the Pyrenees on one side and the Atlantic Ocean on the other, which meant our diet was heavy on fish and vegetables. There was always a connection to someone who had a plot of land. Everyone I knew was growing something one way or another. And it was also easy to walk to the harbors of Bermeo or Mundaka, both small fishing villages, and buy fish that was caught minutes before. It is still that way back home.

If I had to pick my last supper, this would be it. My mom's fish soup, a dish intrinsic to Basque culture—served daily at tables across the region—and a big bowl of simple greens. Of all the recipe advice I seek from my mother, the most frequently asked involve this dish: "What type of fish would you use from this selection?" or "What bread do you add?" Because not all fish is created equal; not all bread is the same. Ultimately, though, the success and extraordinary flavor of the soup will depend on your fish. The fish bones and prawn heads are all indispensable, and I would even go so far as to say that if you cannot find whole fish and prawns (shrimp will do) in your market, then don't bother. That's how important they are. Make friends with your fishmonger and ask if they have some hidden frozen fish heads in the back. Often they do, and these would make a perfect stock when whole fish is out of season and unavailable.

My Mom's Fish Soup

1 whole (2-pound or 1-kg) rockfish or snapper (or a piece of halibut with bones, but ideally use a head-on fish), scales and insides removed and cleaned

1 large bunch (15 g) Italian parsley, plus more chopped for garnish

10 cups (2250 g) cold water

2 pounds (1 kg) whole spot prawns or langoustines, divided

5 tablespoons extra-virgin olive oil, divided

1 large yellow onion, finely chopped (about 2 cups)

1 medium leek (white part only), washed and finely chopped (about ⅓ cup)

1 medium carrot, peeled and finely chopped (about ½ cup)

½ medium green bell pepper, seeded and finely chopped (about ⅓ cup)

2 cloves garlic, minced

2 teaspoons kosher salt

2 heaping tablespoons tomato paste

1 tablespoon *pimiento choricero* paste (optional)

3 ounces (90 g) Sourdough Boules (page 103) or other crusty bread of choice, toasted

One important tip for planning: although not necessary, I recommend you make the soup base a day ahead (without adding the clams, prawn meat, or fish). The flavor will deepen as most soups do overnight. You could even freeze it for up to 3 months. When you are ready to proceed, heat up the base and finish the soup by adding the fresh seafood.

Native to northern Spain, the *choricero* pepper is a variety that gets its name from being the pepper used in making chorizo sausage. The peppers are red, small, and elongated. They are harvested in late summer and hung to dry. You will see them all over many entrances at old Basque farmhouses. The peppers are sold dried but also as a paste in jars. The paste is made by reconstituting dry peppers, then scraping out the inside flesh. The flavor is sweet yet tangy. You can find jarred *pimiento choricero* paste in any specialty shop that sells Spanish products. If you cannot find it, it's OK to omit or add 1 teaspoon of sweet paprika.

MAKES 6 TO 8 SERVINGS

1 Place the whole rockfish and parsley in a large pot. Cover with the water. Cover the pot and bring the water to a simmer over medium-high heat. When the first bubbles rise, impurities will also surface. Skim this foam off, reduce the heat to medium low, cover again, and simmer for 7 minutes, or until the fish is tender. Meanwhile, peel 1½ pounds of the prawns, saving the shells and heads for the stock. Reserve the remaining ½ pound whole prawns for serving.

2 Gently remove the fish from the water onto a large plate. Using a fork, carefully separate the flesh from the bones and skin. It's OK if there are some pin bones in the flesh—you can remove those later when the fish is cool enough to handle. Return the carcass to the pot, add the prawn heads and shells, and simmer for an additional 20 minutes. Strain the fish stock through a fine-mesh sieve into a bowl or pot large enough to hold all the liquid. You should have about 8 cups of stock. Set aside.

½ cup (115 g) txakoli or other dry
   white wine
1 pound (about 2 dozen) clams,
   rinsed in cold water
Piment d'Espelette (optional)

3   Heat 4 tablespoons of the olive oil in another large pot over medium heat. Add the onion, leek, carrot, bell pepper, garlic, and salt and stir. Cook the vegetables for about 10 minutes, or until very tender but not browned. Add the tomato paste, pimiento choricero paste, and toasted bread. Stir everything together. At this point it will look very soft and mushy, which is good. Add the txakoli and let the alcohol cook down for 1 minute. Add the reserved fish stock, cover the pot, and simmer for 20 minutes.

4   Puree the soup base with a food mill or blender. A food mill is my mom's preferred method because it leaves the base slightly textured and avoids incorporating too much air, which can happen when using a high-speed blender, but either method will work. Taste the soup base and adjust with salt if needed, but remember that the clams will have a bit of sea brine in them.

5   Return the blended soup base to the pot and bring to a low simmer over medium heat. Add the clams, cover the pot, and cook until the clams start to open, about 3 minutes. Add the shelled prawn meat and cook for 1 minute. Finally, add the cooked rockfish and stir.

6   Heat the remaining tablespoon olive oil in a large sauté pan over high heat. Add the reserved whole prawns and cook for 1 minute on each side, just until they turn pink. Toasting the prawn shells this way will add a lot of flavor.

7   Ladle the soup into bowls and top each with a few whole prawns, a sprinkle of parsley, and a pinch of piment d'Espelette. Serve hot.

Aioli and Gruyère Tartines

This tartine, or toast, is the perfect accompaniment to my mother's fish soup. You can skip the cheese if you are avoiding dairy and simply toast the bread on its own before slathering the top with aioli.

MAKES 6 SERVINGS

6 slices Sourdough Boules
  (page 103) or other crusty
  bread
6 tablespoons aioli (page 35)
4 ounces (115 g) gruyère cheese,
  coarsely grated

1   Preheat the broiler. Place the bread on a baking sheet, spread each slice with 1 tablespoon aioli, and top with gruyère. Broil until the cheese is melted and bubbling, about 2 minutes. Keep a close eye on it so the cheese doesn't burn. Serve the tartine immediately alongside the soup.

Peppery Greens with Mustard-Honey Vinaigrette

This is such a simple, balanced salad—the spice of the greens is complemented by sweetness from the honey and acidity from the vinegar and mustard. It is one of my favorite ways to dress a green salad. You can make the vinaigrette ahead of time, but be sure to wait and toss it with the greens right before serving so the greens stay crisp.

MAKES 6 SERVINGS

1 tablespoon apple cider vinegar
2 teaspoons honey (preferably
  raw and local)
1 teaspoon whole-grain mustard
1 teaspoon ground coriander
1 teaspoon flaky sea salt
½ teaspoon freshly ground
  black pepper
¼ cup (55 g) extra-virgin olive oil
6 cups tender peppery greens,
  such as arugula, mizuna,
  watercress, or mustard greens

1   Whisk together the vinegar, honey, mustard, coriander, salt, and pepper in a large bowl. Slowly drizzle in the olive oil while whisking to create a creamy emulsion. Add the greens to the bowl and toss with the vinaigrette until well coated. Serve immediately.

VEGETARIAN HARVEST GATHERING

MENU

*Ricotta Gnudi with
Slow-Roasted Tomatoes*

*Roasted Squash Salad with
White Beans, Bread Crumbs,
and Preserved Lemon*

Ginger-Fennel Tonic

Every October on Lopez Island, my friend Hardie Cobbs, an artist, gathers friends and family to help harvest all the apples and pears in her small orchard. The children climb the trees looking for every last piece of fruit, which they later help press and turn into thick, caramel-color cider. There is a lot of bustle and excitement, but we take breaks to brew tea and sit around listening to impromptu banjo sessions. We even turn some of the cider into Salted Apple Cider Caramels (page 322) and Caramelized Apple Galettes (page 117). It's a weekend-long affair on one of the most beautiful islands off the coast of Washington.

"Can I cook for this year's harvest party crowd?" I asked Hardie. She loved the idea. I chose a menu that represents the bounty of late summer and early fall with tomatoes at their peak and the beginning of winter squash. The recipes are hearty, nourishing, and easy to make for a crowd (even in Hardie's tiny island kitchen). I wanted this vegetarian dinner to feel rich and abundant, so I chose more complex dishes that have texture. I often gravitate toward hearty recipes that nod to the comfort of long, slow cooking. For example, the sauce for the *gnudi* has the concentrated depth of tomatoes that have been roasting in the oven for an hour. The roasted squash and bean salad has many hearty, creamy, and crunchy components, making it as visually stunning as it is satisfying.

Many of the time-consuming components, such as slow-roasted tomatoes, white beans, or even gnudi, can be made ahead of time, then finished and assembled right before serving so you can relax and enjoy your guests.

Ricotta Gnudi with Slow-Roasted Tomatoes

These pillowy dumplings are delicate to handle, but that is precisely where their beauty comes from. I recommend mixing and shaping them the night before or early in the morning before serving so they have time to absorb the flour well, which helps them hold together better when cooking. You can make the tomato sauce with canned whole tomatoes (San Marzano are great) instead of slow roasting—just be sure to drain any liquid from the can first.

MAKES 6 SERVINGS

1 To make the gnudi, mix together the ricotta, Parmesan, egg, salt, and nutmeg in a medium bowl. Stir in the brown rice flour and ⅓ cup of potato starch, adding more starch as needed if the dough is too wet. The dough should be light, not too dry, and able to hold together when spooned. Dust a baking sheet with some more brown rice flour. Using a large soup spoon, scoop up some of the dough and gently tap it to release onto the floured baking sheet. You can use a second spoon to help release the dough. Repeat until you have scooped all the dough. Cover the gnudi with plastic wrap and chill in the refrigerator for at least 1 hour and up to 24 hours.

2 To make the slow-roasted tomatoes, preheat the oven to 325 degrees F. Toss the tomatoes, olive oil, sugar, oregano, thyme, and salt together on a baking sheet or in a large roasting pan. Bake for 1 hour, or until the tomatoes have softened and caramelized. Pick out the thyme sprig and discard. If you are not going to use the tomatoes right away, cool completely and store in the refrigerator for up to 5 days.

3 When you are ready to cook the gnudi, fill a large pot with water and bring to a boil over high heat. Keep the gnudi refrigerated until just before cooking. Gently add the gnudi to the boiling water. Reduce the heat to medium so the water simmers but doesn't boil too harshly, as the gnudi may fall apart. Cook in batches if needed. Once the gnudi float to the top, cook for another 2 to 3 minutes (be careful not to overcook or they will disintegrate). Remove the cooked gnudi from the boiling water with a slotted spoon and transfer to your serving platter. Top the gnudi with the roasted tomatoes and more Parmesan.

For the gnudi
1 pound (454 g) whole-milk ricotta

2 ounces (55 g) finely grated Parmesan cheese, plus more for serving

1 large egg, lightly beaten

¼ teaspoon kosher salt

Pinch of freshly grated nutmeg

½ cup (70 g) superfine brown rice flour, plus more for dusting

⅓ to ½ cup (55 g to 80 g) potato starch

For the slow-roasted tomatoes
2 pounds (1 kg) whole cherry tomatoes or halved plum tomatoes

½ cup extra-virgin olive oil

2 teaspoons sugar

2 teaspoons fresh oregano leaves

1 sprig thyme

1 teaspoon flaky sea salt

Roasted Squash Salad with White Beans, Bread Crumbs, and Preserved Lemon

This salad offers a serious combination of flavors and textures while still being simple and uncomplicated. The roasted squash and white beans are buttery, the bread crumbs add texture, and the preserved lemons offer a surprising floral brine. The beans need to soak for a few hours, so plan for that. You can certainly use canned beans instead, but simmering the soaked beans with bay and garlic will ultimately be more flavorful, and the soaked beans retain their texture better than canned ones. My preference is to keep the squash unpeeled if the skin is thin and free of too many hard bumps.

MAKES 6 SERVINGS

1 cup (170 g) dried cannellini beans
1 head garlic, halved crosswise
1 bay leaf
2 pounds (1 kg) kabocha, acorn, or butternut squash, seeded and sliced
½ red onion, sliced ¼ inch thick
2 cloves garlic, peeled
4 tablespoons extra-virgin olive oil, divided
1 teaspoon kosher salt
1 teaspoon freshly ground black pepper
1 teaspoon ground cumin
½ teaspoon sumac (optional)
¼ to ½ teaspoon cayenne or piment d'Espelette
2 slices stale Sourdough Boules (page 103) or other bread of choice
2 tablespoons finely chopped preserved lemon rind (page 48)
1 tablespoon finely chopped Italian parsley
1 tablespoon red wine vinegar
Microgreens or sprouts, for garnish (optional)

1   Place the dried beans in a medium Dutch oven. Cover with water by 2 inches and refrigerate for 8 to 12 hours.

2   Drain the soaking water from the beans and discard. Add more water so the beans are covered by 1 inch. Add the head of garlic and bay leaf to the pot. Bring to a boil over medium heat. Reduce the heat to low and simmer the beans for 45 to 50 minutes, or until tender but not mushy. Drain the beans. Discard the bay leaf and garlic. The beans can be stored in the refrigerator for 1 to 2 days.

3   While the beans are cooking, preheat the oven to 400 degrees F. Toss the squash, onion, garlic cloves, 3 tablespoons of the olive oil, salt, pepper, cumin, sumac, and cayenne together on a baking sheet. Bake the squash for 30 minutes, or until tender and golden brown.

4   Place the bread in a food processor and pulse into chunky bread crumbs. Heat the remaining tablespoon olive oil in a medium sauté pan over medium heat, and add the bread crumbs. Stir until well coated with oil and toasted, about 2 minutes. Toss in the preserved lemon and parsley.

5   Transfer the roasted vegetables to a platter. Top with the beans, bread crumbs, vinegar, and microgreens. Toss everything together and serve lukewarm or at room temperature.

Ginger-Fennel Tonic

This drink is the precursor to ginger beer. Grated ginger is fermented for a few days to create a bubbly, naturally probiotic tonic. The process is similar to creating a sourdough starter by capturing wild yeast and bacteria through water and carbo-hydrates (sugar). It is important to use filtered water here, as chlorine in tap water will prevent bacteria from growing. Note that you will need to start between 4 and 5 days before you plan to serve the tonic. If you do not have 5 days to prepare the ginger bug, you can always use store-bought ginger beer as a "cheat." Make the tonic at least 1 hour before serving so it's nice and chilled.

MAKES 6 SERVINGS

For the ginger bug
1½ cups (340 g) filtered water
5 tablespoons grated unpeeled ginger, divided, plus more depending on length of fermentation
5 tablespoons sugar, divided, plus more depending on length of fermentation

For the tonic
1 teaspoon fennel seeds
6 leaves mint, plus more for garnish
1 cup gin
⅓ cup freshly squeezed lime juice (about 5 limes)
1 lime, cut into 6 wedges

1   On the first day, combine the water, 1 tablespoon of the grated ginger (from about a 1-inch piece), and 1 tablespoon of the sugar in a clean, sterilized glass jar. Stir vigorously and cover the jar opening with cheesecloth, which is best secured with a rubber band. Let the ginger ferment at room temperature (ideally 70 to 75 degrees F) for 24 hours.

2   On the second day, add another tablespoon of the grated ginger and 1 tablespoon of the sugar. Stir vigorously once again, cover with the cheesecloth, and let ferment for another 24 hours. Repeat the process for 3 more days. By the fifth day, the ginger mixture should be fizzy, smell yeasty, and be cloudy and yellow in color. You should have about 2 cups of ginger bug. It is best kept in the refrigerator and fed 1 tablespoon grated ginger and 1 tablespoon sugar once a week.

3   When you are ready to make the tonic, muddle the fennel seeds and mint together in a 4-cup measuring glass. Add the ginger bug, gin, and lime juice and stir. Refrigerate for 1 hour. Strain into chilled glasses and serve with a lime wedge.

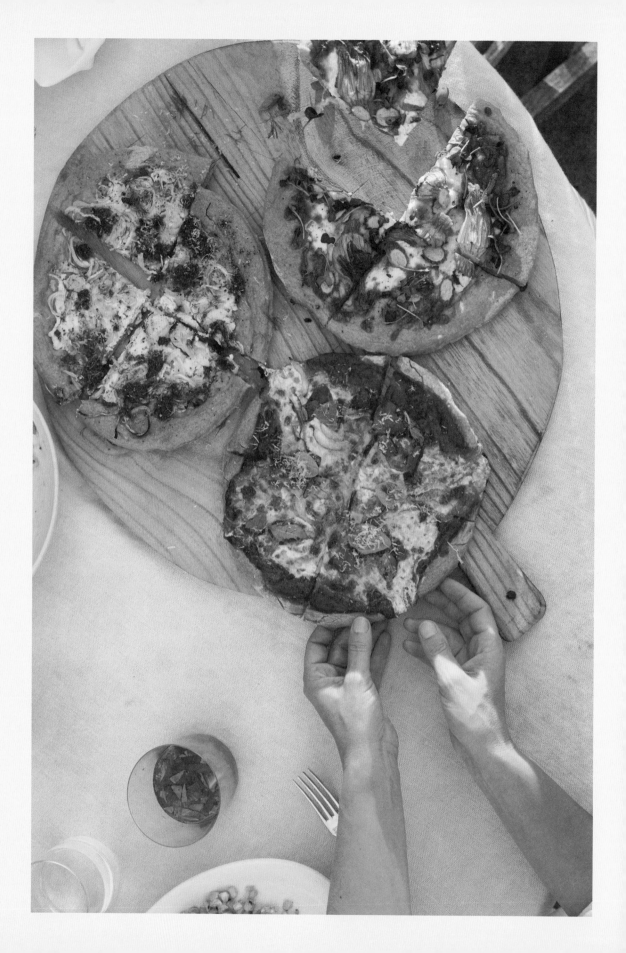

GRILLED BACKYARD PIZZAS

_____

MENU

Pizza Dough

Squash Blossom and Ricotta Pizza

Tomato, Prosciutto, and Red Onion Pizza

Leek, Fennel, and Pesto Pizza

Blistered Corn, Nectarine, and Watercress Salad

Mashed Berries in Lillet

My family cooks outside year-round. Our neighbors across the street, who moved to Seattle from Cape Town, admitted to us that they thought we were a rare breed when they looked out their living room window in the dead of winter to see us standing next to our grill, prepping this or that while the charcoal glowed. They thought it was quite bizarre. But after taking part in some of our block party dinners, they themselves bought a grill and now join us outside on even the most bitter days.

We own a Green Egg, which is a ceramic, egg-shaped charcoal grill that we have owned for over ten years; it has become a staple in our cooking repertoire. It is a dream of ours to eventually build a wood-burning fireplace so we can truly perfect our pizzas, but for now the grill works great. Fire and heat are critical in this process. It might take a few trials to get it right. Too hot and the bottom of the pizza will burn. Not hot enough and it won't get the crispness you need by the time the toppings are cooked. Our trick is to have two cast-iron pizza stones available—one goes on the grill, and the other is a standby in case the first one gets too hot. We find that alternating between the two works great.

You can also bake the pizza in an oven. Be sure to position a cast-iron pizza stone in the bottom third of the oven so the crust gets the most heat. Let the stone preheat for at least fifteen minutes.

Pizza Dough

4½ teaspoons (18 g) active
    dry yeast
5 cups (1125 g) filtered water,
    heated to 110 degrees F
1½ teaspoons sugar
1½ cups (210 g) superfine brown
    rice flour, plus more for
    dusting
1½ cups (210 g) sorghum flour
1 cup (120 g) tapioca starch
¾ cup (120 g) potato starch
4½ tablespoons (45 g) psyllium
    husk powder
2¼ teaspoons kosher salt
1 tablespoon extra-virgin
    olive oil

Note: This pizza dough takes
a little bit longer to cook than
ones made with wheat flour,
so don't fret if you feel like it's
taking a while to bake well. If
you are making a flatbread-type
pizza with delicate ingredients
that cook quickly (such as
zucchini blossoms or sautéed
mushrooms and eggs), I recommend prebaking the dough with
a drizzle of olive oil for about
15 minutes, then adding the
toppings to finish baking.

This versatile dough can be baked or grilled into pizzas, and it
also works well for flatbreads. Three excellent pizza options
follow on pages 257 to 259. Another favorite way I prepare pizza
is brushing it with a generous amount of olive oil; sprinkling with
some flaky salt, cumin seeds, oregano, and piment d'Espelette;
and then grilling it until it's crispy and puffed up.

MAKES ENOUGH DOUGH FOR 6 PIZZAS

1   Put the yeast in a mixing bowl, and pour the warm water over
it while whisking until dissolved. Whisk in the sugar, then let the
yeast activate for 15 minutes, or until frothy.

2   In the bowl of a stand mixer, whisk together the brown rice
flour, sorghum flour, tapioca starch, potato starch, psyllium
powder, and salt. Add the yeast mixture and olive oil, and give
it a stir with a wooden spoon to begin incorporating the flour
and water. With the dough hook, mix for 3 minutes on medium
speed until the dough is smooth. The dough will be wet but
should hold together nicely and have some bounce. Add more
flour or water if needed.

3   Dust a work surface and a baking sheet with brown rice flour.
Transfer the dough to the work surface, lightly dust the top with
more brown rice flour, and cut it into four equal pieces. Roll
each piece into a ball and place on the baking sheet, leaving
at least 3 inches between the balls as they will expand while
they proof. Cover the dough loosely with a clean kitchen towel.
Proof at room temperature for 45 to 60 minutes. You can use
the dough at this point, but if you have the time, transfer the
baking sheet to the refrigerator for at least 6 hours and up to
24 hours. The flavor and chewiness of the dough will continue
to develop this way. If you do refrigerate it, set the dough out at
room temperature for 30 minutes before baking. You can also
freeze the dough at this point, tightly wrapped. Thaw in the
refrigerator overnight.

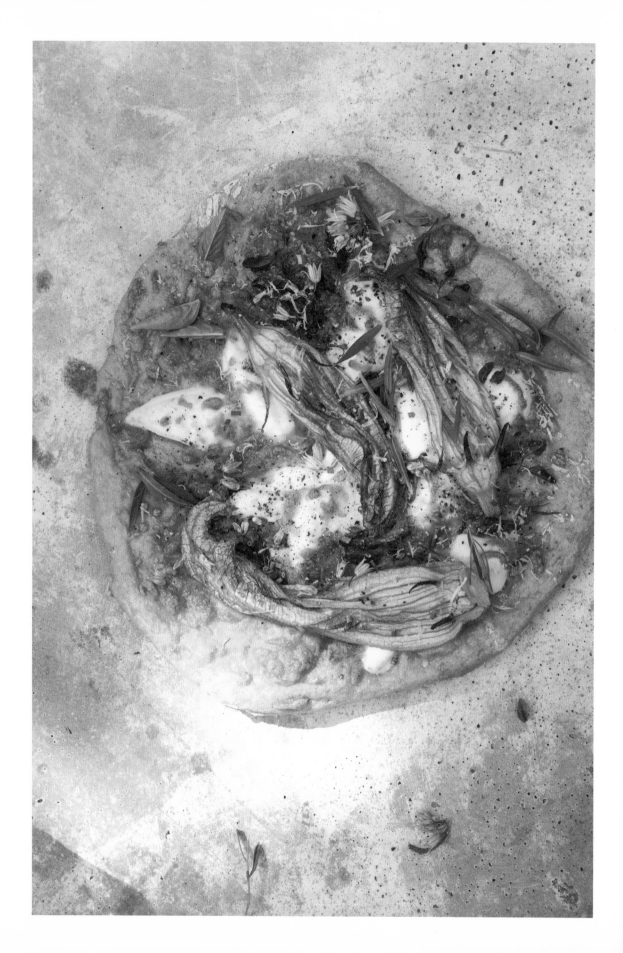

Squash Blossom and Ricotta Pizza

Cornmeal, for dusting

⅛ recipe Pizza Dough (page 254)

¼ cup (55 g) whole-milk ricotta

¼ cup (55 g) shredded mozzarella

3 tablespoons extra-virgin olive oil, divided

2 teaspoons fresh oregano leaves

½ teaspoon freshly ground black pepper

4 to 5 squash blossoms

¼ cup finely grated Parmesan cheese

Squash blossoms have a short season, and they are very delicate. You will most likely find them at your local farmers' market—not at a grocery store—because they are hard to transport and their shelf life is extremely short. I hesitated to include this recipe because it isn't an ingredient you will regularly have on hand, but it is so good. I thought it would be something really special to try when you do get your hands on some. If you cannot find squash blossoms, you can still make this pizza by thinly slicing one summer squash in their place.

MAKES 1 PIZZA

1 Preheat a grill with a pizza stone on it to 500 degrees F. Dust a pizza peel with cornmeal. Place the dough on the pizza peel, and roll it into a 10-inch circle. Give the dough a good shake to make sure it doesn't stick to the peel.

2 Spread the ricotta and mozzarella evenly over the dough, drizzle with 2 tablespoons of the olive oil, and sprinkle with the oregano and pepper. Slide the pizza onto the preheated stone, close the grill lid, and bake for 10 minutes.

3 If there are zucchini stems attached to the blossoms, slice them thinly. Lift the grill lid. Scatter the squash blossoms and any sliced stems over the pizza and drizzle with remaining tablespoon olive oil. Close the lid and finish cooking until the crust is golden brown and the squash begins to caramelize, about 10 more minutes. Transfer the pizza to a platter, top with the Parmesan, and serve immediately.

Tomato, Prosciutto, and Red Onion Pizza

The combination of tomato and prosciutto is a classic for good reason. There is always a bit of controversy about whether the prosciutto should be cooked. Some people like to add the prosciutto after the pizza comes out, letting the heat lightly warm it, and others, like me, prefer my prosciutto cooked. I think it enhances its saltiness. This pizza makes use of my go-to sauce recipe, which is not cooked and tastes quite light. You can also use it as a barely-there pasta sauce.

MAKES 1 PIZZA

For the tomato sauce
1 (14-ounce) can pureed tomatoes (preferably San Marzano)
3 tablespoons extra-virgin olive oil
1 clove garlic, finely minced
1 teaspoon dried oregano
½ teaspoon kosher salt
½ teaspoon freshly ground black pepper

For the pizza
Cornmeal, for dusting
⅙ recipe pizza dough (page 254)
⅓ cup (40 g) shredded mozzarella
1.5 ounces (40 g) fresh mozzarella, torn into 2-inch pieces
6 thin slices prosciutto
¼ cup thinly sliced red onion
Extra-virgin olive oil, for drizzling
2 tablespoons fresh basil leaves, torn into large pieces

1 To make the sauce, stir the tomatoes, olive oil, garlic, oregano, salt, and pepper together in a small bowl. It can be made 1 day in advance and refrigerated in an airtight container. You should have about 2 cups sauce, which is more than you will need for 1 pizza. Measure out ¼ cup of the sauce and set aside. Transfer the remainder to a freezer-safe container and freeze for up to 3 months.

2 When you are ready to make the pizza, preheat a grill with a pizza stone on it to 500 degrees F. Dust a pizza peel with cornmeal. Place the dough on the pizza peel, and roll it into a 10-inch circle. Give the dough a good shake to make sure it doesn't stick to the peel.

3 Spread the reserved ¼ cup tomato sauce over the dough in a circular motion, making sure to leave a ½-inch clean perimeter. (If the sauce spills over the side, it will be difficult to slide the dough on and off the stone.)

4 Top the pizza with the shredded mozzarella, then the mozzarella pieces, prosciutto, onion, and a good drizzle of olive oil. Slide the pizza onto the preheated stone, and close the grill lid. Cook until the crust is golden brown and the cheese is melted. The time will vary depending on the grill, but it should be between 20 and 25 minutes. Transfer the pizza to a platter, top with the basil, and serve immediately.

Leek, Fennel, and Pesto Pizza

This pizza showcases some of my favorite spring produce. It would be equally great with other tender spring vegetables, such as asparagus or baby artichokes. The pesto recipe is my basic go-to, but you can switch things around by using almonds or pistachios instead of pine nuts or by replacing basil with other herbs and tender greens, such as watercress, spinach, or nettles (after they are blanched).

MAKES 1 PIZZA

For the pesto
3 cups packed basil leaves (from about 3 bunches)
3 tablespoons raw pine nuts
1 clove garlic, peeled
1 teaspoon flaky kosher salt
½ cup (125 g) cup extra-virgin olive oil
2 ounces (55 g) finely grated Parmesan cheese

For the pizza
Cornmeal, for dusting
⅛ recipe pizza dough (page 254)
¼ cup (55 g) whole-milk ricotta
½ small bulb fennel, thinly shaved
¼ medium leek (white and light-green parts only), thinly sliced
½ teaspoon freshly ground black pepper
¼ cup finely grated Parmesan cheese

1 To make the pesto, in a food processor, blend together the basil, pine nuts, garlic, and salt to a paste. Scrape the sides of the bowl and pulse one more time. With the machine running, drizzle in the olive oil. Transfer the pesto to a bowl and fold in the Parmesan. The pesto can be made up to 3 days in advance and stored in the refrigerator. You should have about 1 cup pesto, which is more than you will need for 1 pizza. Measure out ¼ cup of the pesto and set aside. Transfer the remainder to a freezer-safe container and freeze for up to 3 months.

2 When you are ready to make the pizza, preheat a grill with a pizza stone on it to 500 degrees F. Dust a pizza peel with cornmeal. Place the dough on the pizza peel, and roll it into a 10-inch circle. Give the dough a good shake to make sure it doesn't stick to the peel.

3 Spread the ricotta evenly over the dough. Scatter the fennel, leek, dollops of the reserved ¼ cup pesto, and black pepper on top. Slide the pizza onto the preheated stone, and close the grill lid. Cook until the crust is golden brown and the cheese is melted. The time will vary depending on the grill, but it should be between 20 and 25 minutes. Transfer the pizza to a platter, top with the Parmesan, and serve immediately.

Blistered Corn, Nectarine, and Watercress Salad

3 ears corn, husked

3 tablespoons extra-virgin olive oil, plus more for brushing

2 ripe yellow nectarines, cut into wedges

1 medium shallot, thinly sliced

2 cups watercress

¼ cup basil leaves, torn

¼ cup mint leaves, finely chopped

¼ cup dill fronds, torn

2 tablespoons freshly squeezed lemon juice

1 teaspoon grainy mustard

½ teaspoon ground cumin

½ teaspoon flaky sea salt

½ teaspoon freshly ground black pepper

In the summertime, when corn is abundant and sweet, my family loves to make this salad, which is fresh and slightly smoky. In the colder months, invent your own salad with at least one grilled ingredient. Options might include halved radicchio grilled directly on the grate or grilling brussels sprouts in a cast-iron pan.

MAKES 6 TO 8 SERVINGS

1 Preheat a grill to 450 degrees F. Brush the corn with a little olive oil and grill it until charred, about 5 minutes on each side. You could also do this in a cast-iron pan over high heat on the stovetop. Transfer to a plate to cool. Once cool enough to handle, run a sharp knife close to the center of the cob to cut the kernels off into a serving bowl. Add the nectarines, shallot, watercress, basil, mint, and dill.

2 In a small bowl, whisk together the olive oil, lemon juice, mustard, cumin, salt, and pepper. Pour over the salad, toss, and serve immediately.

Mashed Berries in Lillet

1 cup whole strawberries
1 cup whole raspberries
2 tablespoons thinly sliced basil
1 (750-ml) bottle Lillet
½ cup (115 g) freshly squeezed
  lemon juice

Lillet is an aperitif wine made from Bordeaux grapes and macerated fruit liqueurs. It is slightly sweet and mixes well with very ripe fruit. Serve chilled. There is a blanc and a rosé version—either will do here.

MAKES 6 SERVINGS

1 Combine the strawberries, raspberries, and basil in a large bowl or pitcher, and muddle them together with the handle of a wooden spoon without turning them into a puree. Pour the Lillet and lemon juice over the fruit, cover with plastic wrap, and refrigerate for at least 4 hours to macerate the fruit. Serve in chilled glasses.

SUNDAY ROASTED CHICKEN

MENU

Buttermilk-Brined Roasted Chicken

Roasted Potatoes the English Way with Tarragon Aioli

Artichoke, Fennel, Sugar Snap Pea, and Parmesan Salad

In the low-light days of winter, Sundays have an especially slow rhythm to them. My usual farmers' market run doesn't feel as anxious as in summer months, when I am navigating crowds and there is so much produce to sort through. The options are few, so I stick to the bare bones of roasted chicken, potatoes, and a salad. Roasted chicken is humble, but bringing the bird to the table on a beautiful platter elevates this moment to something a bit more celebratory—and God knows we need it on winter Sundays.

The potatoes are one of my favorite things about this meal. I learned a trick for cooking them when I lived in London for one summer when I was twelve. The lady of the house cooked her potatoes in duck fat, and she taught me to parboil them first so they could be a bit smashed before baking. More surface for crispy skin, she said. She was right.

Buttermilk-Brined Roasted Chicken

This recipe needs no introduction. If you are avoiding dairy, substitute the quart of buttermilk with water plus the juice of three lemons, then drop the whole squeezed lemons into the brine along with the rest of the herbs and spices. The acidity from the lemons will help compensate for not using the buttermilk.

MAKES 4 TO 6 SERVINGS

4 cups (945 g) cold water, divided

1 yellow onion, quartered

6 cloves garlic, peeled and smashed

1 bunch Italian parsley

1 bunch tarragon

3 tablespoons sugar

3 tablespoons plus 2 teaspoons kosher salt, divided

1 tablespoon whole black peppercorns

1 bay leaf

1 quart (945 g) full-fat buttermilk

1 (3½- to 4-pound) whole chicken

1 tablespoon Aleppo pepper

2 sprigs rosemary

2 sprigs thyme

1 pound (454 g) carrots, cut into 2-inch dice

2 medium red onions, cut into 1-inch-thick wedges

3 tablespoons extra-virgin olive oil

1   Combine 2 cups of the water, yellow onion, garlic, parsley, tarragon, sugar, 3 tablespoons of the salt, peppercorns, and bay leaf in a medium saucepan. Bring to a simmer over medium-high heat and cook until the sugar and salt have dissolved. Transfer the brine into a large bowl or stockpot big enough to fit the chicken. Stir in the buttermilk and remaining 2 cups cold water. Submerge the chicken in the brine, topping off with more cold water if needed. Refrigerate overnight.

2   The next day, remove the chicken from the brine, pat dry, and place on a baking sheet. Place the chicken, uncovered, in the refrigerator for at least 3 hours. This will help dry the skin so it gets crispy when roasted.

3   Preheat the oven to 425 degrees F. Pat dry the chicken once again. Season all sides and the cavity with the remaining 2 teaspoons salt and Aleppo. Stuff the cavity with the rosemary and thyme.

4   Scatter the carrots and red onions on a roasting pan. Place the chicken on top of the vegetables and drizzle with the olive oil, allowing it to coat the vegetables too. Rub the oil all over the chicken skin. Roast the chicken, basting with oil drippings every 20 minutes, for 1 hour, or until an instant-read thermometer inserted in the thickest part of the thigh reads 165 degrees F.

5   Transfer the chicken to a cutting board, and let it rest for 15 minutes before cutting so the juices don't run out. Serve the carved chicken on a platter alongside the roasted carrots and onions.

Roasted Potatoes the English Way with Tarragon Aioli

5 Yukon Gold potatoes (about
   3½ pounds or 1.5 kg), peeled
   and cut into 2-inch cubes
¼ cup (55 g) extra-virgin olive oil
2 teaspoons flaky sea salt
1 teaspoon freshly ground
   black pepper
1 cup tarragon aioli (see Note)

Note: To make tarragon aioli,
follow the recipe for basic aioli
on page 35. Add 2 tablespoons
tarragon leaves when mashing
the garlic and salt together in the
mortar and pestle, and proceed
as directed.

This is my favorite way of cooking potatoes. In the recipe
below, I indicate to peel the potatoes, but if the skin is thin
and free from too many blemishes, you could simply scrub
them and leave the skin on. Also note that even though I call for
Yukon Golds, you could use Russets or any other type of potato.
If you have access to duck fat (many supermarkets stock it in
the freezer section these days), use it instead of the olive oil.
The potatoes will be extra rich and flavorful.

MAKES 6 SERVINGS

1 Preheat the oven to 425 degrees F. Put the cubed potatoes
in a large stockpot or Dutch oven and cover with cold water
by 1 inch. Cover the pot, and bring the water to a boil over high
heat. Cook the potatoes for 5 minutes, reducing the heat to
medium if needed to avoid boiling over. Drain the potatoes in
a colander, shake off any excess water, and return them to the
pot. Put the lid back on, and shake the pot vigorously until the
potatoes are slightly smashed but still whole.

2 Spread the potatoes evenly on a baking sheet and toss
well with the olive oil, salt, and pepper to coat. Bake for 35
to 40 minutes, or until the potatoes are golden brown. They
will be crisp on the outside and soft inside. Serve with the
tarragon aioli.

Artichoke, Fennel, Sugar Snap Pea, and Parmesan Salad

This is a perfect spring salad, but you can make it year-round. Larger artichokes will work, but make sure you only use the very tender hearts (make artichoke soup with the larger leaves). The salad is light and bright—a nice contrast to the rich chicken and potatoes.

MAKES 6 SERVINGS

8 ounces (225 g) sugar snap peas
2 cups (450 g) cold water
½ cup (115 g) freshly squeezed lemon juice
8 baby artichokes (2 pounds or 1 kg)
1 medium bulb fennel
2 cups arugula
¼ cup dill sprigs
¼ cup (55 g) extra-virgin olive oil
1 teaspoon finely grated lemon zest
1 teaspoon flaky sea salt
½ teaspoon freshly ground black pepper
2-ounce (55-g) piece Parmesan cheese

1 Slice the sugar snap peas diagonally ½ inch wide and place in a serving bowl or platter.

2 Pour the water and lemon juice into a large bowl. Prepare the artichokes by trimming the stems, cutting off the pointed tips, and removing any tough outer leaves. Slice the artichokes thinly, preferably with a mandoline. Immediately drop the artichokes into the lemon water and swish around to stop oxidization. Thinly slice the fennel with the mandoline and drop into the lemon water.

3 Drain the artichokes and fennel, and add them to the bowl with the sugar snap peas. Add the arugula, dill, olive oil, lemon zest, salt, and pepper and toss everything together. Using a vegetable peeler, shave the Parmesan into strips, and let them fall on top of the salad. Serve immediately.

CELEBRATING WITH OYSTERS AND STEAK

_____

MENU

Oysters with Champagne Mignonette

The Perfect Steak with Garlic and Red Chili Flakes

Shaved Asparagus, Cucumber, and Pistachio Salad

I have many food memories involving my grandmother Miren, but the way she cooked steak is ingrained in my brain. Steak and oysters weren't something we ate often, mostly during a celebratory affair or when out-of-town family came by to visit. My grandfather's brother, *el tío* Julian, was also a great cook and a professional pastry chef in a nearby town. He was always in charge of bringing oysters or lobster. He was a large, burly man with a sophisticated palate and larger-than-life personality, but he was also a bit scruffy and messy. He would shuck the oysters and prepare very simple mignonettes to accompany them.

The meat usually came from Fernando, *el carnicero* (the butcher), who had his shop across the street from our family's pastry shop. My grandmother was gentle in her ways but also a demanding customer, and Fernando knew he could not hide the freshest cuts from her. She brought the paper-wrapped steak home; seasoned it with salt, finely minced garlic, and parsley; and let it rest until all the other elements of the meal were prepared. Then the steaks were quickly seared in a hot pan with olive oil. On the rare side was her preference, always.

It all felt somehow humble but also luxurious—because this meal was reserved for certain occasions and gatherings, there was an air of celebration and elegance that I still feel when I opt to make it. It allows for a surprisingly relaxed and unfussy evening, but one that is as decadent as it is beautiful.

Oysters with Champagne Mignonette

About 2 dozen oysters (see instructions)

For the champagne mignonette
½ cup (115 g) champagne vinegar
1 medium shallot, finely minced
½ medium Fresno chili, seeded and finely chopped
¼ teaspoon flaky sea salt

If you have never shucked an oyster, you might feel intimidated by it. We have all heard stories about people stabbing themselves, and it's true that one must study the anatomy of the oyster to understand where its shell hinge is and how to run your knife through it. But I promise you will eventually become a pro. Follow the instructions below on how to buy, store, and shuck.

Champagne mignonette is the classic accompaniment for oysters, but you can experiment with others that include finely diced apple, horseradish, or radishes. Acid, such as vinegar or lemon juice, is important. But at the end of the day, you can also serve them as is so you can enjoy their full briny flavor.

MAKES 6 SERVINGS

For the oysters

1 I recommend buying oysters from a trusted source on the same day you plan to serve them. I tend to buy 4 oysters per person, but it really depends on your crowd and their appetites. Get a variety of oysters from different locales and ask the oyster seller about what's available.

2 As soon as you bring the oysters home, rinse them in cold water and scrub any debris from the shells. Keep them refrigerated in a bowl with ice at around 40 degrees F until you are ready to shuck them. Remember that oysters are alive and need to breathe, so do not place them in a sealed container. Discard any open oysters that don't close back up when you tap them and any with cracked shells and exposed flesh. They are most likely dead and spoiled.

3 Use a shucking knife to open the oysters—don't use a regular paring knife because if you slip, you will really hurt yourself. Shucking knifes are stocky with a slightly rounded point and not as sharp. Wear a shucking glove or hold a sturdy kitchen towel in your opposite hand to protect you from any slips. It's not hard to open an oyster, but it is a slippery process. Hold the oyster so the cup side faces down and the flat side faces up. $\longrightarrow$

4 Slip the tip of the shucking knife between the top and bottom shell right beside the hinge, and wiggle firmly to pry the shells apart. Keep the oyster level so the juices—or liquor, as it's also known—stay in the shell, then run your knife along the length of the shell to release the top from the bottom. Wipe the knife, then run it under the oyster to release it from its muscle. Now it is ready to slurp.

5 Prepare a platter with a base of rock salt or ice, and nestle the shucked oysters on top. Serve with the mignonette.

6 Combine the vinegar, shallot, chili, and salt in a small bowl and refrigerate for at least 1 hour to pickle the shallot. Serve alongside the oysters.

The Perfect Steak with Garlic and Red Chili Flakes

2½ pounds (1,135 g) rib eye, New York strip, T-bone, or tri-tip steak

2 teaspoons kosher salt

1½ teaspoons freshly ground black pepper

⅓ cup (75 g) extra-virgin olive oil, divided

5 cloves garlic, thinly sliced

2 teaspoons red pepper flakes or piment d'Espelette

2 tablespoons sherry or red wine vinegar

2 teaspoons flaky sea salt

1 tablespoon finely chopped Italian parsley

Picking the right steak is practically an art. Rib eye, porterhouse, T-bone, and New York strip are the standards most people consider when choosing steak, but there is a new wave of whole-animal butchers that are making us rethink the traditionally cheaper cuts of meat. I also find it fascinating that butchers in different areas of the country have different cuts and names. The best thing to do is find a good local butcher and see what they recommend. Personally, I love tri-tip, which is a cut I learned about from friends in California but couldn't find on the East Coast when I lived in Florida. It is a less expensive steak but very flavorful, and it works great with high heat.

Timing is key. It is best to get your steak the day before cooking. Place it, unwrapped, on a tray in the refrigerator, which will dry the surface and create a crispy crust when cooked. Remove from the refrigerator an hour before cooking.

Seasonings can make or break the flavor. Steak needs quite a bit of salt, so don't skimp. Season the steak generously at least an hour before cooking it for more intense flavor. Peppers and chili powders pair well with it, as do robust herbs like rosemary.

Choose your fat. I know most people don't like to cook with olive oil, but I grew up using it for everything—even a steak that cooked over high heat. Finishing with salted butter, even flavored salted butter, is a great option also.

MAKES 6 SERVINGS

1 Remove the steak from the refrigerator 1 hour before cooking. Pat dry with paper towels, and season all sides with the kosher salt and black pepper.

2 When you are ready to cook, heat a large cast-iron or heavy stainless steel pan over high heat for 5 minutes, until the pan is very hot. Pat dry the steak with paper towels to remove any additional moisture drawn out by the salt. Rub the steaks with 2 tablespoons of the olive oil, then carefully add them to the hot pan. Don't crowd the steaks; if your pan is not large enough, cook them in batches. Once the steaks hit the pan, $\longrightarrow$

do not move them. Let the steak cook until the first side is caramelized, 3 to 4 minutes, then flip over with tongs and finish cooking on the other side for another 3 to 4 minutes. For medium rare—my personal preference—cook the steak to 125 degrees F (insert an instant-read thermometer through the side into the center of the steak). Transfer the steaks to a cutting board, and let them rest for 15 minutes before slicing.

3   Meanwhile, heat a medium sauté pan over medium heat. Add the remaining olive oil, garlic, and red pepper, and cook until the garlic is golden, about 2 minutes. Remove the pan from the heat and carefully add the sherry—the oil will splatter. Swirl the pan to incorporate.

4   Cut the steak into 1-inch-thick slices. Arrange on a platter and pour the hot garlic oil all over. Sprinkle the flaky sea salt and parsley over the top and serve.

Shaved Asparagus, Cucumber, and Pistachio Salad

To me, steak and asparagus are an ideal combination, so I developed this salad to accompany the perfect steak. There is something so proper about the pairing; it's a departure from your typical sautéed stalks.

MAKES 6 SERVINGS

1   Trim the tough bottoms of the asparagus. The best way to find where the bottoms become tough is to hold the ends of each spear between your fingertips and gently bend it to see where it naturally wants to snap. After all the asparagus are trimmed, use a vegetable peeler to thinly shave them into a large bowl. Leave the tender tips whole or cut them in half. Add the cucumber, spinach, lettuce, parsley, chives, and shallot and toss.

2   In a small bowl, whisk together the olive oil, whey, lemon juice, salt, and pepper. Pour the dressing over the salad and toss gently. Scatter the chopped pistachios and chive blossoms on top. Serve immediately.

12 ounces (340 g) green asparagus
1 medium cucumber, thinly sliced
2 cups spinach leaves
2 cups chopped red or green
   leaf lettuce
¼ cup Italian parsley leaves
¼ cup finely sliced chives
1 medium shallot, thinly sliced
¼ cup (55 g) extra-virgin olive oil
1 tablespoon yogurt whey,
   full-fat buttermilk, or watered-
   down yogurt
1 tablespoon freshly squeezed
   lemon juice
1 teaspoon flaky sea salt
½ teaspoon freshly ground
   black pepper
¼ cup shelled pistachios,
   coarsely chopped
Chive blossoms (optional)

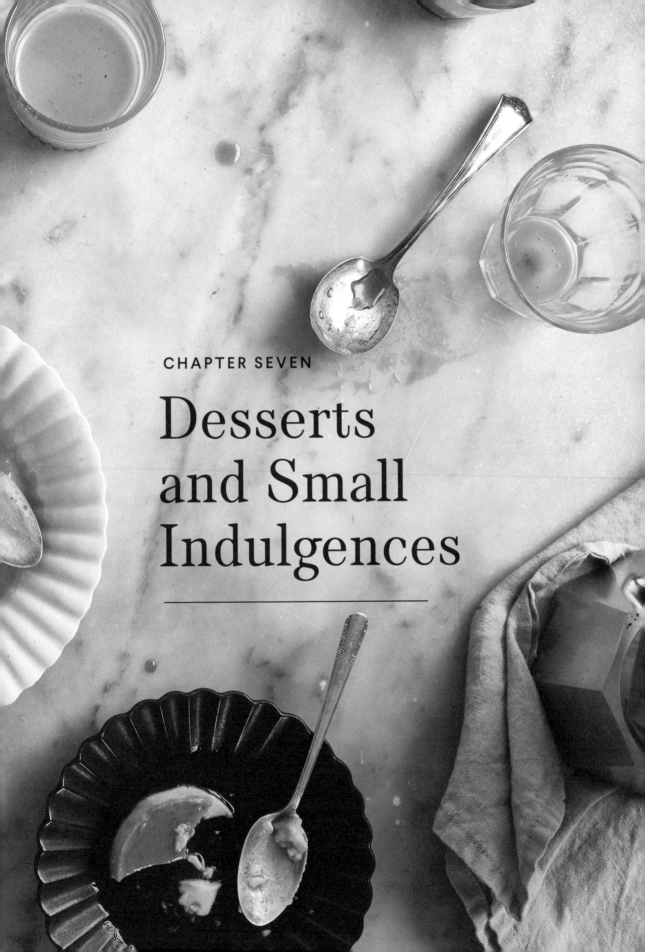

CHAPTER SEVEN

Desserts and Small Indulgences

When I have a group of friends around my table, I never want the evening to end. This chapter is all about lingering after dinner with desserts that are small indulgences. The Spanish tradition of *sobremesa* is central to a meal shared with friends or family, perhaps equally as important as the food. It refers to the conversation that surrounds the table, the endless type that leaves empty glasses of wine, stems of roasted pears and some bits of crumble, a sliver of chocolate, small cups of espresso, a cheese plate with homemade *membrillo* (quince paste), or the last bite of peach hibiscus sorbet.

Some of the recipes in this chapter are as simple and easy as buttermilk panna cotta with summer fruits. Some are a little more involved such as frozen custard with raspberry and hazelnut crunch, which makes for a beautifully elegant dessert. But my goal is for all to feel light yet indulgent.

A treat after the meal gives you the perfect excuse to draw out the evening—a sweet finale that caps all the best dinners. This course doesn't have to be lavish—save that richness for the conversation. Allow instead for something thoughtful with a hint of sweetness, making space to continue the connections as darkness falls, to enjoy coffee or tea, and a little something extra to delight.

Building a Cheese Plate

I want to begin by saying that I don't believe in too many rules or not-to-do lists. In general, serve the cheeses that make you happy. You don't like blue? Then no blue. You like it big and wild? Then make it big and wild. I am listing some of my personal preferences and rules of thumb, and you can take what works for you.

1 Keep it simple. In general, I don't serve more than five cheeses. Why five and not four? Well, I like odd numbers when I plate and serve. There is no logic really; it's just something I do.

2 Ask your cheesemonger. Let's support our local cheese shops! They will talk to you for hours about different makers and what goes well with what, so please pay them a visit. I try to keep things as local as possible, but I have to say I'll always throw Idiazábal on my cheese plate—I am Basque after all, and it's a crowd-pleaser.

3 Keep it varied. I always have a mixture of soft, semi-soft, and aged cheeses, as well as a variety of milk sources—cow, sheep, and goat. I will usually have a triple cream made from cow's milk, a soft goat round or triangle, a deeply veined blue (the yellower and bluer the better), a smoked aged sheep (Idiazábal), and a really sharp cheddar.

4 Tally the number of guests. I purchase about 3 ounces (85 g) of cheese per person. It's the right amount for after dinner when it's more about nibbling than filling up.

5 Determine when to serve it. I grew up with a cheese plate always being served at the end of a meal. It was only when I moved to the US that I noticed people serving cheese plates as an opener to a meal. I still prefer cheese afterward.

6 Select accompaniments. What to serve with your cheese is also a personal preference. Again, I like to keep it simple: cheese, quince paste (or other fruit paste), fresh fruit, nuts, and raw honey. That is all. I leave the cured meats and charcuterie to start a meal, and end it with a cheese plate.

Below is a list of some of my favorite cheeses at the moment, but also ask your cheesemonger about their favorites to build your own list.

BEECHER'S FLAGSHIP. Beecher's is an institution in Seattle, and I have to include it in this list. Its cheddar is semi-hard, nutty, and made with cow's milk.

CYPRESS GROVE'S HUMBOLDT FOG. With an ash stripe running through its center, this is a recognizable American goat cheese and one my friends go crazy for. It is fudgy and softens quickly at room temperature. It is a very mild goat cheese—even people who think goat cheese is too gamy love it.

SMOKED IDIAZÁBAL. This is the quintessential Basque cheese made with raw sheep's milk from Latxa or Carranza sheep. When I was a kid, in the beginning of spring, our local sheep-herder walked the sheep up to the higher pasture where sheep spent all summer and had their babies. The milk collected was turned into lightly pressed and lightly aged cheese, which was then smoked by the fire to dry. We eat Idiazábal with quince paste and walnuts all winter long.

ROGUE CREAMERY'S SMOKEY BLUE. Produced in Oregon with raw cow's milk, this blue cheese is cold-smoked for 16 hours over hazelnuts. It has a semi-soft texture and is very smooth.

MEADOW CREEK'S GRAYSON. Produced in Virginia, this is a cheese similar to Taleggio that would fall into the stinky category. It has an orange rind and fudgy interior that softens quickly at room temperature. It is nutty, buttery, and grassy.

PECORINO ORO ANTICO. This is a sheep's milk pecorino made in Tuscany. Firm, flaky, nutty, and salty, it is the perfect sliver to eat with fruit.

Quince Paste

---

1 medium lemon

4 large quinces

Sugar (same amount as pureed quince)

Assorted cheeses, for serving (page 288)

Quince is one of my favorite fall fruits. It grows well in colder northern climates where apples and pears do well. It is inedible when raw, but its sweet and intense fragrance of something in between pineapple and chamomile brings me so much joy. The shape resembles somewhat an amorphous pear with yellow fuzzy skin and dry white flesh. It must be always cooked, but be careful because it is hard to peel and cut. I have cut myself before while peeling quince.

Quince paste, or *dulce de membrillo* as it is called in Spain, is a sweet, thick jelly made from quince and sugar. It is a staple on any cheese plate in Spain. A slice of bread topped with Idiazábal cheese and membrillo was one of my favorite childhood after-noon snacks. It is sold in many cheese shops, but I still make it every fall when I get my hands on some quince. If you cannot find quince, you could also make apple paste following this method, although the cooking time will be less since apples are softer than quince.

MAKES 16 SERVINGS

1 Cut the lemon in half, and juice it directly into a medium pot filled with water.

2 Peel, core, and quarter the quince. Cut each quarter in half and submerge in the lemon water to stop the quince from oxidizing. Bring the water to a simmer over medium heat, then cook the quince until it is very tender, about 20 minutes. Drain the quince in a colander, then transfer it to a food processor or blender and puree until smooth.

3 Place a bowl on a kitchen scale, tare it, and weigh the amount of pureed quince you have. Weigh the same amount of sugar as puree.

4 Combine the puree and sugar in a medium heavy-bottomed pot over medium-low heat and stir. Cook, stirring often, until the quince is very thick and has turned a deep golden-orange color, about 1 hour. As the sugar cooks, it has a tendency to splatter, so be very careful and wear protective gloves if necessary. If you are unsure of when the quince paste is done, take a small sample with a teaspoon and place in the freezer for a minute to have a sense of what the texture will be once it cools. The cooled membrillo should be thick—you should be able to cut it with a knife. Continue cooking until it reaches this consistency.

5 Lightly grease a 9-inch square pan, and line the bottom with parchment paper. Spoon the membrillo into the prepared pan, and smooth the top with a spatula. Be careful because it will be extremely hot. Let the paste cool at room temperature. It should be soft but firm. I like to store it in the refrigerator wrapped in plastic wrap, where it keeps for months.

6 Serve the paste at room temperature with assorted cheeses.

Amama
Miren's Flan

1½ cups (300 g) sugar, divided
1 medium lemon
2 cup (450 g) whole milk
1 vanilla bean, split lengthwise
   and seeds scraped
1 cinnamon stick
¼ teaspoon kosher salt
4 large whole eggs plus
   2 egg yolks

There was always milk simmering in a large stockpot in our family's pastry shop. It was raw milk from the dairy up the street—a dairy that had no more than a handful of cows but enough milk to drive down the hill and into town in large metal canisters for my grandmother to pasteurize. The milk that was pasteurized in the morning was used to make custard the next day. Day in, day out. There was little waste, but the days in which there was leftover milk, my grandmother made *arroz con leche* (rice pudding) or flan. Both were prepared very simply, with cinnamon, vanilla, and a touch of lemon zest. I couldn't decide on which I preferred, but because I shared the recipe for the arroz con leche in my blog in 2008, when I started it, I am sharing the recipe for her flan here.

I like to use 4-ounce ceramic or metal ramekins for the flan, but you can also use different molds, such as a metal Charlotte mold, an 8-inch cake pan, or even a loaf pan. This recipe is easy to multiply to serve a large crowd. Plan to make this a few hours before you are going to serve it so it has time to chill. Ideally make the night before.

MAKES 6 SERVINGS

1   Preheat the oven to 300 degrees F. Set six ramekins on a work surface. Bring a teapot of water to a boil.

2   Heat a medium stainless steel sauté pan or saucepan over high heat. Sprinkle 1 cup (200 g) of the sugar evenly in the pan and wait until the sugar starts to melt. Continue cooking until it starts turning light amber, then you can stir it with a wooden spoon to distribute any uneven clusters of sugar. Cook until the sugar turns a deeper amber color, and immediately pour the caramel into the ramekins. Swirl the caramel around so it coats the bottoms of the ramekins. Set aside.

3   Cut strips of lemon rind with a vegetable peeler, then combine them with the milk, vanilla bean and seeds, cinnamon stick, and salt in a medium saucepan. Warm the milk over medium heat until it begins to appear frothy, but do not let it boil. Remove the pan from the heat and steep for 15 minutes to infuse the flavors. $\longrightarrow$

4   Whisk together the whole eggs, egg yolks, and remaining ½ cup sugar in a large bowl. Pour in the warm milk and immediately whisk together until smooth. Strain the custard through a fine-mesh sieve into a clean bowl, preferably with a spout, then pour the custard into the molds. Place the molds in a deep baking pan and bring to the oven. Pour boiling water into the pan so it reaches halfway up the molds. Cover the pan with aluminum foil, then bake for 50 to 55 minutes, or until the flan is set in the center. Remove the pan from the oven, then remove the molds from the water bath. Let the flan cool at room temperature for 15 minutes, then refrigerate for at least 4 hours, or until set.

5   To serve, gently loosen the sides of the custard with a knife. Make sure you serve the flan in a dish deep enough to hold the caramel sauce. Invert the dish on top of the mold, flip it over carefully, and gently tap once until you hear the flan release from the mold. Lift the mold off, letting all the caramel run over the top and onto the sides. Serve immediately.

Apricots in Honey and Saffron

10 ripe but firm apricots, halved
   and pitted
½ cup (115 g) dry white wine,
   such as txakoli or sauvignon
   blanc
¼ teaspoon flaky sea salt
4 green cardamom pods,
   cracked
Small pinch of saffron (about
   6 threads)
¼ cup honey (preferably raw and
   local)
3 tablespoons coarsely chopped
   pistachios
Vanilla ice cream, whipped
   cream, or whole-milk vanilla-
   flavor yogurt, for serving
   (optional)

Sometime in the mid-aughts, I discovered Diana Henry's *Crazy Water, Pickled Lemons*, one of the first cookbooks I found that introduced Middle Eastern flavors into traditional Western cooking. And even though I had grown up on the Atlantic coast of Spain not far from Mediterranean ingredients, it was through Diana's writing and style that I began to see these traditional influences with a new perspective. I consider this recipe of baked apricots with saffron very much inspired by Diana's books and recipes.

MAKES 6 SERVINGS

1 Preheat the oven to 350 degrees F. Place the apricots cut side up in a baking dish. Pour in the white wine and sprinkle in the salt, cardamom, and saffron. Stir around. Drizzle the honey all over the apricots, then bake for 20 to 25 minutes, or until the apricots are tender but not falling apart. The juices and honey should make a nice syrup.

2 Serve the warm apricots with the chopped pistachios and a scoop of ice cream or a dollop of thick yogurt on top.

Chocolate, Olive Oil, and Citrus Cake

The thinnest sliver of chocolate cake at the end of a meal can settle an evening like nothing else can. Just a little bit sweet, a little bit salty, and a little bit tart. The air in this cake, which comes from the whipped egg whites, collapses as the cake cools, giving the crust a crunch to pair with the tender, brownie-like interior.

MAKES ONE 9-INCH CAKE

½ cup (115 g) extra-virgin olive oil, plus more greasing

5 large eggs, at room temperature

8 ounces (225 g) 85 percent bittersweet chocolate, coarsely chopped

1 cup (200 g) granulated sugar, divided

1 lemon, zested and juiced

1 orange, zested and juiced

1 teaspoon flaky sea salt

Powdered sugar, for dusting

Whipped cream, for serving (optional)

1   Preheat the oven to 350 degrees F. Position a rack in the center of the oven. Brush the bottom and sides of a 3-inch-deep and 9-inch-diameter cake pan with olive oil. Cut a large piece of parchment and fit it into the bottom of the pan and all the way up the sides.

2   Separate the eggs by cracking the egg whites into the squeaky-clean bowl of a stand mixer and the egg yolks into a small bowl. Room-temperature egg whites whip better and hold more air than cold ones, so the cake will turn out best if you let them sit on the counter while you prep everything else.

3   Place the chocolate in a heatproof bowl, and find a medium pot the bowl will fit in nicely. Fill the pot halfway with water, and bring it to a simmer over medium-low heat. Place the bowl on top and gently melt the chocolate. Once all the chocolate is nearly melted, remove the pot from the heat and allow the residual heat to melt the remaining pieces. If your chocolate is too hot, let it cool for 5 minutes before adding the rest of the ingredients. Whisk in the olive oil, ½ cup of the granulated sugar, 2 teaspoons lemon zest and 1 tablespoon juice, 2 teaspoons orange zest and 1 tablespoon juice, salt, and finally, the egg yolks. Set aside. The texture might feel a bit gritty, but that's OK.

4   Whip the egg whites in the stand mixer fitted with the whisk attachment on high speed. You could also do this by hand or with an electric beater. When the whites are fully foamed and turn an opaque white, 1 to 2 minutes, slowly sprinkle in the remaining ½ cup sugar, with the mixer running, until they become glossy and firm, 4 to 5 minutes. $\longrightarrow$

5   Fold a third of the whipped whites into the chocolate base until fully incorporated. You can be as aggressive as needed at this stage because you are just lightening the base. Gently fold in the remaining whites, this time being careful not to deflate them too much as this air from the meringue is what will help the cake rise. If you have a few streaks of white left through the batter, it's OK. Pour the batter into the prepared cake pan and bake for 40 minutes. The top will crack and deflate as it cools. Let the cake cool for 15 minutes in the pan.

6   Lift the cake out with the parchment and place on a serving plate. Dust with powdered sugar and serve with whipped cream.

Roasted Pears with Seed Crumble

Pears that are juicy yet firm withstand a long roasting time, and I tend to gravitate toward Bosc because of their long, elegant stems. They should be a dark golden-caramel color with skin with some snap. If they are soft enough that you can slide a spoon into them, the mouthfeel will be delectable. The seed crumble will add everything else. The ice cream is included mostly for indulgence but can be skipped if you would prefer.

MAKES 6 SERVINGS

4 medium (1½ pounds or 750 g) ripe yet firm Bosc pears or other pear of choice
¾ cup (150 g) sugar, divided
7 tablespoons water, divided
4 tablespoons (55 g) unsalted butter, divided
2 tablespoons (50 g) honey (preferably raw and local)
1 medium lemon
1 medium orange
1 cinnamon stick
1 vanilla bean, split lengthwise and seeds scraped
¾ teaspoon kosher salt, divided
1 cup (135 g) mixed seeds (I use pumpkin, sunflower, and sesame)
Vanilla ice cream (optional)

1 Preheat the oven to 400 degrees F. Peel the pears, cut them in half lengthwise, and remove the cores with a teaspoon.

2 In a 10-inch cast-iron pan over medium-high heat, combine ¼ cup of the sugar, 4 tablespoons of the water, 2 tablespoons of the butter, honey, 4 strips of lemon rind plus its juice, 4 strips of orange rind plus its juice, cinnamon stick, vanilla bean and seeds, and ¼ teaspoon of the salt. Cook and stir until the sugar dissolves. Remove the pan from the heat, and gently place the pears in the syrup cut side down. Bake for 45 minutes, basting the pears with the liquid every 15 minutes. The liquid will turn to caramel and the pears a light amber color. If you want the pears to be a bit darker after they come out of the oven, you can heat the pan over high heat for a minute. The caramel will reduce further and the pear color will deepen.

3 While the pears are roasting, prepare the seed crumble. Line a baking sheet with parchment paper. Toast the seeds in a skillet over medium heat until fragrant, about 2 minutes. Combine the remaining ½ cup sugar, 3 tablespoons water, 2 tablespoons butter, and ½ teaspoon salt in a small saucepan. Give the mixture a stir, then cook undisturbed over medium-high heat until it turns a deep amber color, being careful not to burn it. Remove the saucepan from the heat, add the toasted seeds, and stir together with a spatula. Spread the mixture over the parchment paper as evenly as you can, and let it cool completely. It will harden as it cools. Cut the crumble into uneven pieces. It can be made 3 days in advance and stored in an airtight container at room temperature.

4 Serve the pears topped with the seed crumble and vanilla ice cream, then drizzle with the caramel from the cast-iron pan.

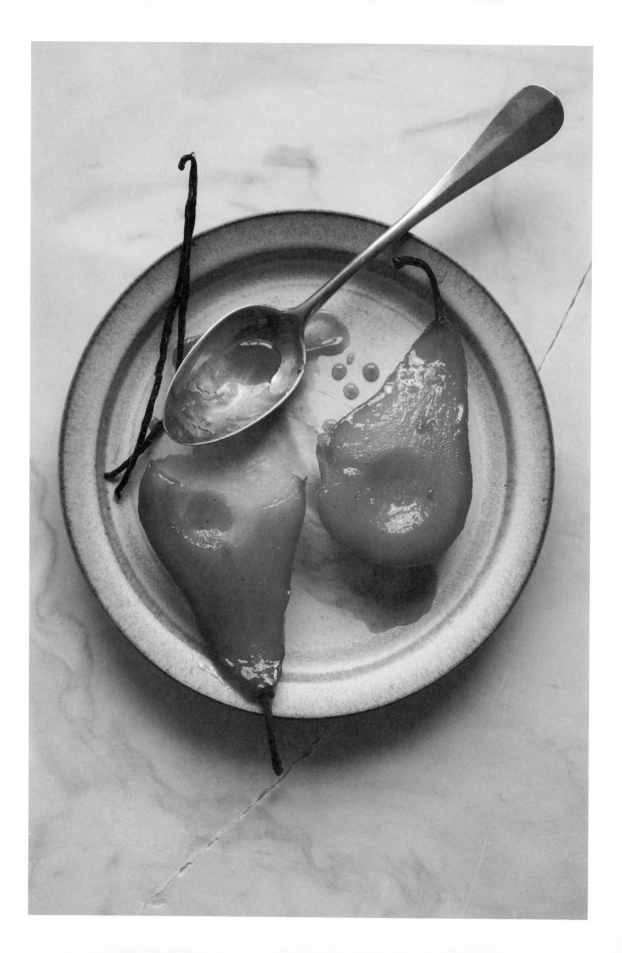

Buttermilk Panna Cotta with Summer Fruits

Panna cotta is one of the easiest yet most elegant desserts you can make. It is essentially gelled heavy cream, and achieving the right consistency can be a fine balance—you don't want it to be too stiff, but it should hold its shape. Because panna cotta is sweet and rich, I always find it needs an acidic balance, whether that is by way of lemon or buttermilk or yogurt or a lightly sweetened rhubarb compote.

MAKES 6 SERVINGS

1 cup plus 2 tablespoons (235 g) cold water
2 teaspoons powdered gelatin
2 cups (225 g) heavy cream
½ cup plus ⅓ cup (165 g) sugar, divided
1 vanilla bean, split lengthwise and seeds scraped
1 cup (115 g) full-fat buttermilk
1 medium lemon
1 stalk rhubarb, cut into ½-inch dice (about 1 cup)
2 peaches, sliced
2 apricots, sliced
1 cup (125 g) strawberries, hulled and halved
1 cup (125 g) raspberries

1 Put 2 tablespoons of the water in a small bowl, and sprinkle the gelatin over the surface. Set aside, and let the gelatin bloom for 5 minutes.

2 Combine the heavy cream, ½ cup of the sugar, and vanilla bean and seeds in a small saucepan, and bring to a simmer over medium heat until sugar dissolves, about 3 minutes. Remove the pan from the heat and whisk in the bloomed gelatin until dissolved. Pour the mixture into a large bowl, remove the vanilla bean, and let the cream cool. When it feels cool to the touch, whisk in the buttermilk, cover the bowl, and chill in the refrigerator for at least 2 hours. The panna cotta should be set.

3 Combine the remaining 1 cup water and remaining ⅓ cup sugar in a medium saucepan over medium heat. Peel two strips of lemon rind with a vegetable peeler and add to the pan. Cook until the sugar is dissolved. Add the rhubarb and cook for a couple of minutes, until tender but not falling apart. Transfer the rhubarb with syrup into a bowl ,and let it cool. Toss in the peaches, apricots, strawberries, and raspberries and chill for 1 hour.

4 To serve, spoon the panna cotta into wide bowls, pour the syrup over the top, and scatter the fruit around. Serve immediately.

Chocolate Cream with Yogurt, Cocoa Nibs, and Raspberries

This easy dessert was inspired by a dinner I had at Reynard in Brooklyn a couple of years ago. The chocolate cream is essentially crème anglaise that is set with gelatin and then blended to incorporate air and lightness.

MAKES 6 SERVINGS

1 tablespoon cold water
1 teaspoon powdered gelatin
6 ounces (170 g) 70 percent bittersweet chocolate, finely chopped
2 cups (225 g) heavy cream
¼ cup (50 g) sugar
½ teaspoon flaky sea salt
5 egg yolks
½ cup (115 g) whole-milk Greek-style yogurt
½ vanilla bean, split lengthwise and seeds scraped
1 cup (125 g) raspberries
2 tablespoons cocoa nibs

1   Put the water in a small bowl, and sprinkle the gelatin over the surface. Set aside, and let the gelatin bloom for 5 minutes.

2   Place the chocolate in a large bowl, and set a fine-mesh sieve over it. Set aside.

3   Combine the heavy cream, sugar, and salt in a medium saucepan over medium heat. In a medium bowl, whisk the egg yolks. When the cream comes to a simmer, pour it over the yolks while whisking constantly. Pour this mixture back into the pan and cook over low heat, stirring constantly with a wooden spoon or a spatula, until it thickens to the consistency of melted ice cream (it should coat the back of the spoon). Do not let the custard boil or it will curdle.

4   Remove the pan from the heat, and immediately add the bloomed gelatin to the custard. Whisk to dissolve. Pour through the fine-mesh sieve (to strain any egg pieces) and over the chocolate. The heat of the custard will begin melting the chocolate. Use an immersion blender to mix the custard and chocolate and incorporate air. Alternatively, you can blend in a high-speed blender or whisk by hand. We want to add as many air bubbles as we can at this point so the chocolate cream will be airy when it cools.

5   Transfer the chocolate cream to a clean bowl. Cover the surface of the cream with plastic wrap, gently pressing against it to prevent a skin from forming. Chill the cream for at least 1 hour. It should be smooth and silky.

6   To serve, whisk the yogurt and vanilla seeds together in a small bowl. Scoop a large tablespoon of yogurt onto a plate, and spread it with the back of the spoon. Using a separate spoon, scoop 2 large tablespoons of chocolate cream and spread over the yogurt with the back of the spoon. Top with raspberries and cocoa nibs, and serve immediately.

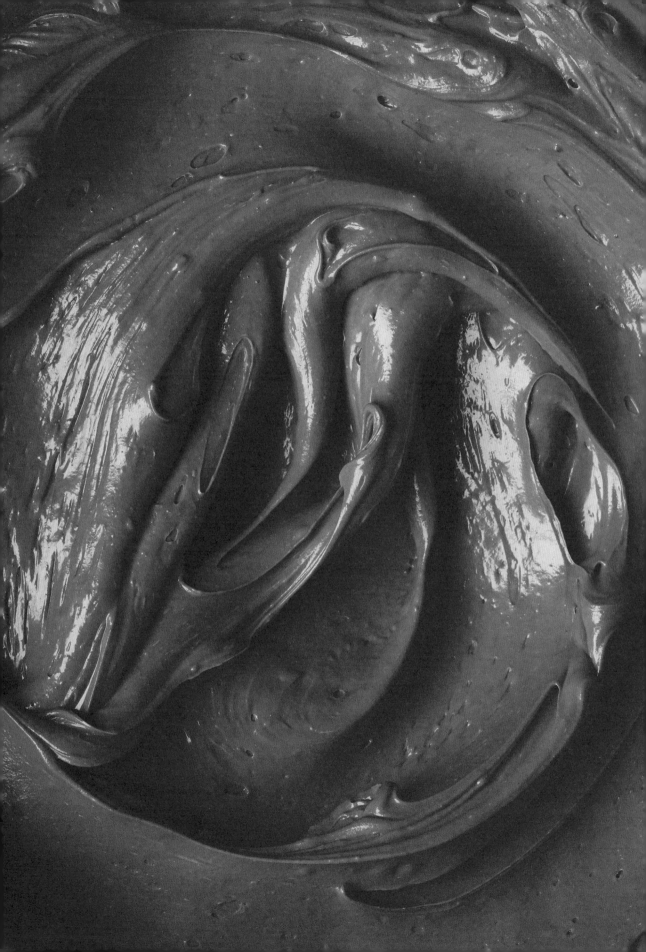

Peach and Hibiscus Sorbet

1 cup (225 g) water
2 tablespoons dried hibiscus
½ cup (100 g) sugar
4 medium (about 1¾ pounds or 795 g) very ripe peaches, peeled and diced
½ cup (115 g) freshly squeezed lemon juice
⅛ teaspoon sea salt

In late summer, peaches are so juicy and ripe that I want to carry them home from the farmers' market gently nestled between towels and bubble wrap. Any minor trauma to the peach and it turns brown in an instant. But that moment *just* before the peach is overripe, that's when you want to make this sorbet. I love the sweetness of this sorbet balanced by the sour hibiscus. You can buy dry hibiscus petals in bulk at tea shops or apothecaries. Its ruby-red color tints the sorbet a deep pink that is irresistible.

MAKES 1 QUART

1 Place the bowl of an ice cream maker in the freezer 24 hours prior to churning.

2 Combine the water and hibiscus in a small saucepan. Bring to a simmer over low heat and let steep for 5 minutes. Stir in the sugar and continue cooking until it dissolves. Strain the syrup into a bowl and set aside to cool completely.

3 Combine the peaches, lemon juice, salt, and hibiscus syrup in a high-speed blender. Puree the mixture and transfer to a bowl. Chill completely in the refrigerator for at least 4 hours.

4 Pour the sorbet base into the ice cream maker bowl, then process according to manufacturer's instructions until thick, usually 15 to 20 minutes. Spoon the sorbet into a freezer-safe container, cover with a lid or plastic wrap, and freeze until solid. Alternatively, if you don't have an ice cream maker, you can freeze the puree in a bowl until solid and whisk it every 20 minutes or so to incorporate some air. Set the sorbet out at room temperature for 5 minutes before scooping.

Espresso and No-Churn Honey Ice Cream

2 cups (450 g) cold heavy cream

1 vanilla bean, split lengthwise and seeds scraped

4 egg yolks

½ cup (200 g) wildflower honey

½ teaspoon flaky sea salt

6 to 8 shots freshly brewed espresso or French press coffee

My advice to those who do not enjoy baking or making dessert: brew some great espresso and add a scoop of good-quality vanilla ice cream. Affogato never fails. It feels timeless and elegant. This recipe is a variation of affogato, and it also offers you a chance to make ice cream without an ice cream machine.

MAKES 6 TO 8 SERVINGS

1 Line a loaf pan with plastic wrap, leaving a few inches of overhang.

2 In a large bowl, whisk the cream and vanilla seeds to soft peaks. You can do this in a stand mixer with a whisk attachment at high speed for about 1 minute, or if you are like me, whisk by hand with some elbow power for about 3 minutes. Refrigerate the cream while you proceed with the recipe.

3 In the bowl of a stand mixer, whip the egg yolks on high speed until they are pale and thick, about 5 minutes. In the meantime, bring the honey and salt to a boil in a small sauce-pan. Reduce the speed to low, and add the warm honey into the yolks in a steady stream. Increase the speed to high and continue whipping until the bowl feels cool to the touch, about 5 minutes.

4 Remove the whipped cream from the refrigerator, giving it a whisk if it looks like it has deflated, and gently fold it into the yolks until no more streaks of cream are visible. It should be thick. Spoon the ice cream base into the prepared pan. Cover with the overhanging plastic wrap and freeze for at least 4 hours, or until solid.

5 When you are ready to serve, line up six espresso cups or small glasses and add a scoop of the vanilla ice cream into each one. Pour the hot espresso over the top and serve immediately.

Frozen Raspberry Custard with Hazelnut Crunch

Here is another ice cream recipe that doesn't require an ice cream machine—it's a *semifreddo* of sorts. The ripple of berries through lemony custard and salty hazelnut crunch sprinkled throughout are heaven. It comes together rather quickly but needs some time to freeze. In a pinch, you can always crush up some of your favorite store-bought salty almond shortbread cookies in place of the crunch, although it can be made several days in advance to save time on the day of serving.

Better yet, double the hazelnut crunch recipe and freeze half of it before baking. When you are ready to use it, you don't even need to thaw it out. Spread it, frozen, on a baking sheet and bake for maybe 3 minutes longer. The crunch is great on ice cream or sautéed fruit, and it can be a lifesaver for those impromptu dessert cravings and dinner parties.

MAKES 6 TO 8 SERVINGS

For the hazelnut crunch
½ cup (70 g) whole hazelnuts
½ cup (50 g) almond flour
⅓ cup (50 g) superfine brown
    rice flour
¼ cup (50 g) sugar
½ teaspoon flaky sea salt
¼ cup (55 g) cold unsalted
    butter, cut into ½-inch pieces

For the raspberry custard
1½ cups (180 g) raspberries
½ cup plus 2 tablespoons (125 g)
    sugar, divided
5 egg yolks
⅓ cup (75 g) freshly squeezed
    lemon juice (from 2 to 3 juicy
    lemons)
1½ cups (340 g) cold heavy cream

1 First, make the hazelnut crunch. Preheat the oven to 325 degrees F. Place the hazelnuts on a baking sheet and toast for 15 minutes, or until fragrant. Place them in a kitchen towel and rub together to loosen their skins. Pick out the peeled hazelnuts (it's OK if some still have a little skin) and transfer to a cutting board. When they are cool enough to handle, roughly chop them. Set aside to cool completely.

2 In a medium bowl, whisk together the almond flour, brown rice flour, sugar, and salt. Add the butter, and using clean hands, rub it into the flour mixture with your fingertips until it resembles coarse sand. Add the cooled hazelnuts and toss together.

3 Increase the oven temperature to 350 degrees F. Spread the hazelnut mixture evenly on a baking sheet lined with parchment paper and bake for 15 minutes, or until golden brown, stirring the crunch halfway through baking. Let the crunch cool completely, then break any large pieces into smaller ones. The hazelnut crunch can be made up to 5 days in advance and stored at room temperature tightly wrapped.

4   Next, make the custard. Line the bottom and sides of a 10-inch springform pan with parchment paper or plastic wrap. Combine the raspberries and 2 tablespoons of the sugar in a medium saucepan over medium-high heat, and cook until the sugar dissolves and the raspberries burst, about 2 minutes. If the raspberries are on the dry side and don't break down, use a fork to lightly mash them. Transfer to a bowl and let cool to room temperature.

5   Bring a small pot of water to a simmer. In the bowl of a stand mixer, whisk together the egg yolks, remaining ½ cup sugar, and lemon juice. Set the bowl over the simmering water and continue whisking for 7 to 8 minutes, or until the egg mixture is pale, frothy, and thick—it should coat the back of a spoon. Don't let the water boil aggressively as it can curdle the eggs. Once thick, return the bowl to the mixer and attach the whisk. Whip on high speed until the bowl feels cool to the touch, about 7 minutes.

6   Meanwhile, whip the heavy cream to soft peaks, about 2 minutes. Once the egg mixture is cool, gently fold the whipped cream in with a spatula. You want to keep in as much air as possible while folding. Finally, fold in the mashed raspberries, creating a nice swirl throughout, but avoid turning the custard completely red.

7   Pour a third of the custard into the prepared pan, top with a third of the hazelnut crunch, then add another layer of custard, topped by another layer of hazelnut crunch, and finish with the custard. Save the remaining hazelnut crunch for topping. Cover the pan with plastic wrap and freeze for at least 4 hours.

8   To serve, remove the pan from the freezer, release spring to unmold the custard, and unwrap. Place on a serving platter. Run a sharp knife under hot water and cut into slices. Serve with a sprinkle of the remaining hazelnut crunch.

Orange and Brown Butter Madeleines

½ cup (115 g) unsalted butter, plus more for greasing
3 large eggs
½ cup (100 g) granulated sugar
2 teaspoons finely grated orange zest
1 teaspoon vanilla extract
¾ cup (90 g) superfine brown rice flour
½ cup (50 g) almond flour
3 tablespoons (25 g) tapioca starch
½ teaspoon baking powder
½ teaspoon kosher salt
Powdered sugar, for dusting

There is something very familiar yet effortlessly classic about finishing dinner with straight-out-of-the-oven madeleines. These ones are scented with orange and nutty brown butter. Serve them hot with a generous dusting of powdered sugar and a shot of *amaro* or *orujo de hierbas*.

MAKES 16 LARGE MADELEINES OR 3 DOZEN MINIS

1   In a small saucepan over medium-high heat, melt the butter until the milk solids start to caramelize, turn foamy and a little brown, and smell nutty, about 5 minutes. Pour the brown butter into a bowl and set aside to cool.

2   Combine the eggs, granulated sugar, orange zest, and vanilla in the bowl of a stand mixer. Whip the mixture on high speed with the whisk attachment until thick and very pale, about 5 minutes. Remove from the mixer and sprinkle in the brown rice flour, almond flour, tapioca starch, baking powder, and salt. Gently fold the ingredients together with a spatula, trying to keep as much air as possible in the batter.

3   When you don't see any streaks of flour left, pour in the brown butter and fold to incorporate. Again, try to be gentle to keep as much air as possible. Transfer the bowl to the refrigerator and chill for 1 hour.

4   Preheat the oven to 425 degrees F. Grease a madeleine pan with a little melted butter. Fit a pastry bag with a medium plain tip (about ½ inch in diameter), or use a large spoon to move batter into the mold or even a ziplock bag with the tip cut. Fold the top edges of the pastry bag outward, and when the batter is chilled and solid, scoop it with a spatula into the bag. Unfold the edges and twist the bag in your hand to pipe the batter into the madeleine molds, filling them nearly to the top.

5   Place the pan in the oven, reduce the temperature to 375 degrees F, and bake for 12 to 15 minutes, or until the madeleines are golden brown, set in the center, and develop a "bump." Carefully unmold the madeleines and dust with powdered sugar. They are best eaten right away.

Salted Hazelnut Butter Truffles

8 ounces (225 g) 70 percent
chocolate, coarsely chopped
¼ cup (55 g) salted butter or
cultured butter (page 24)
1 cup (225 g) creamy hazelnut
butter (page 28)
1½ teaspoons flaky sea salt
1 teaspoon finely grated
orange zest
1 vanilla bean, split lengthwise
and seeds scraped
Finely chopped hazelnuts,
for rolling
Cacao powder, for rolling

I always like to have a small little bite or petit four at the end of the meal—an after-dessert treat. Serve these truffles alongside a shot of espresso or liqueur. You can even make them vegan by substituting the butter with coconut oil (they will be slightly softer, though, so keep them refrigerated at all times).

MAKES 20 TRUFFLES

1 Place the chocolate and butter in a heatproof bowl. Fill a medium saucepan with about 2 inches of water and bring to a simmer over high heat. Reduce the heat to low and position the bowl over the saucepan. Stir the chocolate and butter until melted.

2 Remove the bowl from the pan, wiping the bottom of any condensation. Be careful that no water gets inside the bowl. Stir in the hazelnut butter, salt, orange zest, and vanilla seeds. Cover and chill the chocolate mixture until it is set and scoopable, about 2 hours.

3 Place the hazelnuts on a plate or tray. Using a 1-inch ice cream scoop or a tablespoon, scoop out balls of the chocolate, then roll them in the chopped hazelnuts or cacao powder until coated (I like to make half of each). Store the truffles in an airtight container in the refrigerator until ready to serve, where they will keep for 1 week. Or freeze, tightly wrapped, for up to 1 month; just thaw in the refrigerator overnight before serving.

Salted Apple Cider Caramels

Wrap a few of these caramels in a small bag for dinner guests before they leave your house. The buzz of the night will linger, and they will be able to remember your hospitality and all that happened with a touch of sweet nostalgia. Note that you will need a candy or instant-read thermometer for this recipe.

MAKES 64 CARAMELS

¼ cup (55 g) cultured butter (page 24) or unsalted butter, cut into 1-inch pieces, plus more for greasing
1 quart (950 g) apple cider or unfiltered apple juice
1 cinnamon stick
1 vanilla bean, split lengthwise and seeds scraped
1 cup (200 g) light brown sugar
½ cup (100 g) granulated sugar
½ cup (115 g) crème fraîche (page 26)
1½ teaspoons flaky sea salt, plus more for topping

1 Grease an 8-inch-square pan with a little bit of butter. Line the bottom and sides of the pan with two sheets of parchment paper.

2 Combine the apple cider, cinnamon stick, and vanilla bean and seeds in a medium saucepan, then bring to a boil over medium heat. Continue cooking until the apple cider is reduced to ½ cup, which will be thick and syrup-like. This might take up to 30 minutes, so be patient. Remove the cinnamon stick and vanilla bean from the pan.

3 Add the sugars, crème fraîche, and butter to the pan and stir together. Insert a candy thermometer. Cook the caramel, undisturbed, over medium heat until it reaches 260 degrees F. Remove the pan from the heat, add the salt, and stir well.

4 Pour the caramel into the prepared pan, and let it cool to room temperature. Transfer to the refrigerator for 1 hour to harden before cutting.

5 Place the caramel block on a cutting board. Use a very sharp, oiled chef's knife to cut the block into 1-inch squares. Sprinkle a tiny bit of flaky sea salt on each caramel. You can serve the caramels on a plate, or wrap them in small squares of parchment paper. The wrapped caramels will keep for 1 week in the refrigerator.

Acknowledgments

This book was made possible because of so many generous friends and colleagues. Thank you to Jen Utley for helping extrude the essence of my journey. Thank you to my editor Susan Roxborough and designer Anna Goldstein. Thanks to production editor Bridget Sweet and copyeditor Rachelle Longé McGhee. Judy Linden, my agent, thanks always for your patience and support.

Thank you to my generous friends: Dorothee Brand for the most beautiful portraits, Jenn Elliott-Blake and Jordan Carlson for your advice and impeccable taste, Hardie Cobbs and Carolina Silva for letting me crash at your beautiful homes.

Thank you to my aunt Bego Ayarza for financially backing the video series *A Cook's Remedy* when you knew you would never see a penny back. And Genevieve Pierson, for making the story come to life on film.

Thanks to all the testers that invested time in helping me perfect the recipes: Jen Utley, Becky Dale, Hardie Cobbs, Deb Achak, Kara Hoey, Sally Shintaffer, Aysegul Sanford, Melina Hammer, Vanessa Palomo, Justine Katjar, April Boyer, Jill Haapaniemi, Tanya Protasenya, Devin Pearsall, Anne Foszcz, Belinda Chang, Rachel Demy, Kate McKenna, Jessica Leone, Kelsi Leitz, Jessica Angel, Rena Williams, Emma Galloway, Diemuth Pemsl, Nicole Hoffman, Lentine Alexis, Deb Zener, Beth King, Terisa Means, Alison Bell, Naomi Tran, Alycia Noe, Carrie McCleary, Lisa Posatska, Susanna Marinetti, Ginny Early, Kimberley Hasselbrink, Jenny Choi, Elizabeth Rollins, Danica Roig, Ashley May, Allison Crollard, Klara Heuscher, Katy Ionis, Karen Torres, Kate Marks Roseiro, Lauren McDuffie, Andrea Salzbrenner, Tonya Veilleux, Jim Henkens, Mary Piepmeier, Sarah Lock, Diane Melano, Victoria Thomas, Melissa Wilson-Shaw, Xochtil Jaime, Anitra Sweet, Erin Mullen, Candance Wilson, and Cecilia Stoute.

Thanks to all of you who have followed my blog and Instagram since the very beginning.

Thank you to my family in the Basque Country: *amatxu*, *aitatxu*, Jokin, *eta* Jon. *Eskerrik asko*. And my family in Seattle: Chad, Jontxu, and Mirentxu. I love you.

Online Resources

Below are some of my favorite ceramists who have become good friends throughout the years. Many of their pieces are featured in this book. I'm so grateful for their creations for helping make my work more beautiful. Also listed are some of my favorite resources for homewares and ingredients.

CERAMICS

Akiko Graham
AkikosPottery.com

Astier de Villatte
AstierdeVillatte.com

Baker Potter
BakerPotter.com

Christiane Perrochon
ChristianePerrochon.com

Clam Lab
ClamLab.com

Colleen Hennessey Clayworks
ColleenHennessey.net

Dorotea Ceramics
DoroteaCeramics.com

Elephant Ceramics
ElephantCeramics.com

Helen Levi Ceramics
HelenLevi.com

Henry Street Studio
HenryStreetStudio.com

Janaki Larsen
JanakiLarsenCeramics.com

K. H. Würtz
KHWurtz.dk

Luna Ceramics
Instagram.com/lunaceramics

Mud Australia
MudAustralia.com

Natasha Alphonse Ceramics
AlphonseStudio.com

KITCHEN AND HOME

ABC Carpet & Home
ABCHome.com

Brook Farm General Store
BrookFarmGeneralStore.com

Glasswing
GlasswingShop.com

Herriott Grace
HerriottGrace.com

March SF
MarchSF.com

Marine Area 7
MarineArea7.com

The Primary Essentials
ThePrimaryEssentials.com

Roman & Williams Guild NYC
RWGuild.com

Staub
StaubUSA.com

PANTRY

Arrowhead Mills
ArrowheadMills.com

Authentic Foods
AuthenticFoods.com

Bob's Red Mill
BobsRedMill.com

La Tienda
Tienda.com

Index

NOTE: Page numbers in *italic* refer to photographs.

A

aioli
    Aioli and Gruyëre Tartines, 240, *242*
    basic recipe for, 35
    Roasted Potatoes the English Way with Tarragon Aioli, 269, *270–271*
Apple Cider Caramels, Salted, 322, *323*
Apple Cider Yeast Doughnuts, 130–131, *133*
apples
    Bircher Muesli with Poached Rhubarb and Hazelnuts, 74, *75*
    Braised Chicken with Apples and Cider, *204*, 205
    Caramelized Apple Galette, *116*, 117
    Radicchio, Apple, and Celery Root Salad with Buttermilk–Poppy Seed Vinaigrette, 233, *233*
    Spicy Chicken Salad with Apple, Celery, and Pickled Vegetables, *150*, 151
apricots
    Apricots in Honey and Saffron, 299, *299*
    Buckwheat Sweet Yeast Bread with Dried Apricots and Walnuts, *108*, 109
    Buttermilk Panna Cotta with Summer Fruits, *306*, 307
    Coconut Granola, 72, *73*
    One-Bowl Apricot and Olive Oil Cake, 128, *129*
Artichoke, Fennel, Sugar Snap Pea, and Parmesan Salad, *272*, 273
Asparagus and Avocado Soup, Simple, *156*, 157
Asparagus, Cucumber, and Pistachio Salad, Shaved, *282*, 283
author's personal story, 1–3
avocados
    Avocado, Smoked Salmon, and Cucumber on Toast, *80*, 81
    Crispy Chickpeas with Rice, Sweet Potatoes, Avocados, and Greens, 188, *189*
    Crunchy Romaine Salad with Soft Eggs and Feta, 168, *169*
    My Niçoise Salad, *182*, 183
    Simple Asparagus and Avocado Soup, *156*, 157
    Winter Salad with Roasted Radicchio, Avocados, and Hazelnut Dukkah, 148, *149*

B

baking recipes, 97–143
    Apple Cider Yeast Doughnuts, 130–131, *133*
    Caramelized Apple Galette, *116*, 117
    Cinnamon Buns, 78, *79*
    Fig, Taleggio, and Pine Nut Tart, *122*, 123

Pie Dough 3-2-1, 114–115
Plum Frangipane Tart, 112, *113*
Puff Pastry with Cultured
    Butter, *118*, 119–121
Tomato and Romesco Tart,
    180, *181*
    See also breads; cakes
Banana Bread with Sunflower
    Seed Icing, 136, *137*
beans. *See* legumes
beef
    Beef Stock, *52*, 54
    Braised Beef Ragù with
        Tagliatelle, *231*, 232
    Perfect Steak with Garlic
        and Red Chili Flakes, The,
        279–280, *281*
    Spaghetti and Meatballs,
        196–197, 198
Beet and Lentil Salad with
    Tahini and Preserved Lemon
    Dressing, Shaved, *154*, 155
Berries in Lillet, Mashed, 265, *265*
beverages
    Ginger–Fennel Tonic, 249
    Ginger–Turmeric Milk, 66, *67*
    Mashed Berries in Lillet,
        265, *265*
    Peach Txakoli Cocktail, 219,
        221
    Shrubs and Drinking
        Vinegars, *46*, 47
    Spicy Carrot–Grapefruit
        Juice, 68, *69*
binders, 7
Bircher Muesli with Poached
    Rhubarb and Hazelnuts, 74, *75*
Biscuits, Flaky Caramelized
    Onion and Fennel, *138*,
    139–140, *141*
Biscuits, Strawberry, 140
bread crumbs, homemade, 198
Bread Salad, Tomato, Corn, and,
    164, *165*
breads
    Banana Bread with Sun-
        flower Seed Icing, 136, *137*
    Black Olive, Caraway, and
        Honey Yeast Bread, 110, *111*

Buckwheat Sweet Yeast
    Bread with Dried
    Apricots and Walnuts,
    108, 109
gluten-free bread baking
    tips, 105
gluten-free flours, substitut-
    ing wheat flour for, 6
Gluten-Free Sourdough
    Starter, *58*, 59–61
Nordic Rye-Style Seed
    Bread, *100*, 101–102
Sourdough Boules, 103–104
    See also toast and open-
    faced sandwiches
breakfast, 63–95
Broccoli Rabe and Fried Eggs,
    Lentil and Root Vegetable
    Stew with, *194*, 195
broths. *See* stocks and broths
Brown Butter and Orange
    Madeleines, 318, *319*
Brown Butter Cake, Roasted
    Squash, *134*, 135
Buckwheat Crêpes with
    Chocolate–Hazelnut Butter,
    92, *93*
Buckwheat Sweet Yeast Bread
    with Dried Apricots and
    Walnuts, *108*, 109
Buns, Cinnamon, 78, *79*
Buttermilk-Brined Roasted
    Chicken, *266*, 268, *270–271*
Buttermilk Dressing, Peas and
    Ham with, 160, *161*
Buttermilk Panna Cotta with
    Summer Fruits, *306*, 307
Buttermilk-Poached Salmon
    Salad with Herb, Leek, and
    Caper Dressing, 152, *153*
Buttermilk–Poppy Seed
    Vinaigrette with Radicchio,
    Apple, and Celery Root Salad,
    233, *233*
butters
    Chocolate–Hazelnut Butter,
        29, *31*
    Cultured Butter, 24, *25*
    Simple Nut or Seed Butter,
        28

C
cakes
    Chocolate, Olive Oil, and
        Citrus Cake, *300*, 301–302
    Gâteau Basque, 124–125,
        126–127
    One-Bowl Apricot and Olive
        Oil Cake, 128, *129*
    Parsnip and Ginger Cake
        with Cultured Butter
        and Crème Fraîche Icing,
        142–143, *143*
    Roasted Squash Brown
        Butter Cake, *134*, 135
Candied Pepitas, 171
Caramelized Apple Galette,
    116, 117
Caramelized Onion and Fennel
    Biscuits, Flaky, *138*, 139–140, *141*
Caramelized Peaches, Sourdough
    Waffles with, *90*, 91
Caramels, Salted Apple Cider,
    322, *323*
Caraway, Black Olive, and Honey
    Yeast Bread, 110, *111*
carrots
    Roasted Carrot and Cashew
        Soup, 158, *159*
    Roasted Carrots with Red
        Lentil Hummus, 176–177,
        178–179
    Spicy Carrot–Grapefruit
        Juice, 68, *69*
Cashew and Roasted Carrot
    Soup, 158, *159*
Cashew Cream, *76*, 77
Cauliflower, Swiss Chard,
    and Hazelnut Pasta, Roasted,
    192, *193*
Celebrating with Oysters and
    Steak, 275–283
Celery, Apple, and Pickled
    Vegetables, Spicy Chicken
    Salad with, *150*, 151
Celery Root and Parsnip Mash,
    Crispy Snapper with, 199,
    200–201

Celery Root, Radicchio, and Apple Salad with Buttermilk–Poppy Seed Vinaigrette, 233, *233*

Champagne Mignonette, Oysters with, *276*, 277–278, *278*

cheese plates, 288–289, *290–291*

Cheese Toast, Squash, Leek, and Potato Soup with, *190*, 191

Cherries with Coconut Granola, Roasted, 72, *73*

chicken
Braised Chicken with Apples and Cider, *204*, 205

Buttermilk-Brined Roasted Chicken, *266*, 268, *270–271*

Chicken and Seafood Paella on an Open Fire, 214–215, *216–217*

Chicken Stock, *52*, 53

Spicy Chicken Salad with Apple, Celery, and Pickled Vegetables, *150*, 151

Chickpeas, Crispy, with Rice, Sweet Potatoes, Avocados, and Greens, 188, *189*

chocolate
Buckwheat Crêpes with Chocolate–Hazelnut Butter, 92, *93*

Chocolate Cream with Yogurt, Cocoa Nibs, and Raspberries, 308, *309*

Chocolate–Hazelnut Butter, 29, *31*

Chocolate, Olive Oil, and Citrus Cake, *300*, 301–302

Salted Hazelnut Butter Truffles, *320*, 321

Cider and Apples, Braised Chicken with, *204*, 205

Cinnamon Buns, 78, *79*

Coconut Granola with Roasted Cherries, 72, *73*

Coconut Milk, 21

Corn, Nectarine, and Watercress Salad, Blistered, *262*, 263

Corn, Tomato, and Bread Salad, 164, *165*

Crème Fraîche, 26, *27*

Crêpes with Chocolate–Hazelnut Butter, Buckwheat, 92, *93*

Cucumber, Avocado, and Smoked Salmon on Toast, *80*, 81

Cucumber, Shaved Asparagus, and Pistachio Salad, *282*, 283

Cultured Butter, 24, *25*

Custard with Hazelnut Crunch, Frozen Raspberry, 314–315, *316–317*

D

desserts and small indulgences, 285–323

Detox Broth with Swiss Chard, Turmeric, *70*, 71

dinners, 173–207

Doughnuts, Apple Cider Yeast, 130–131, *133*

Drinking Vinegars and Shrubs, *46*, 47

Dukkah, 40, *41*

E

Eggplant and Green Tomato Salad, Grilled, 218, *220*

eggs, 11
Baked Eggs in Piperrada, 86, *87*

Crunchy Romaine Salad with Soft Eggs and Feta, 168, *169*

Egg Tostada with Fennel, Radishes, and Yogurt, 88, *89*

Lentil and Root Vegetable Stew with Broccoli Rabe and Fried Eggs, *194*, 195

Mushrooms and Eggs, *166*, 167

My Niçoise Salad, *182*, 183

Soft-Cooked Eggs with Dukkah and Bitter Greens on Toast, *84*, 85

Spicy Lamb Sausage with Yogurt, Herbs, and Fried Egg, *202*, 203

Espresso and No-Churn Honey Ice Cream, 312, *313*

F

fats, 8

Fennel and Caramelized Onion Biscuits, Flaky, *138*, 139–140, *141*

fennel bulb
Artichoke, Fennel, Sugar Snap Pea, and Parmesan Salad, *272*, 273

Egg Tostada with Fennel, Radishes, and Yogurt, 88, *89*

Leek, Fennel, and Pesto Pizza, 259

Melon, Serrano, Fennel, and Ricotta Salata, 163

Tortilla de Patatas with Romaine, Fennel, and Green Olive Salad, 184–185, *186–187*

Fennel–Ginger Tonic, 249

Fig, Taleggio, and Pine Nut Tart, *122*, 123

Figs, Radicchio, Pickled Radishes, and Pepitas, Black Rice Bowl with, *170*, 171

fire, tips for building, 215

fish
Avocado, Smoked Salmon, and Cucumber on Toast, *80*, 81

Buttermilk-Poached Salmon Salad with Herb, Leek, and Caper Dressing, 152, *153*

Crispy Snapper with Root Veggie Mash, 199, *200–201*

Fish Stock, *52*, 55

My Mom's Fish Soup, *236*, 238–239

My Niçoise Salad, *182*, 183

Slow-Roasted Salmon with Fennel, Citrus, and Harissa, 206, *207*

Flan, Amama Miren's, *296*, 297–298

flatware, 222, *225*

flours, 5–7

    gluten-free, substituting wheat flour for, 6

    nut, making your own, 20

Flower and Herb Mayonnaise, 35

flowers, decorating with, 223, *224*

Frangipane Plum Tart, 112, *113*

Fruits, Buttermilk Panna Cotta with Summer, *306*, 307

G

Galette, Caramelized Apple, *116*, 117

Garden and the Sea, The, 237–243

Garlic Aioli, Roasted, 35

Gâteau Basque, 124–125, *126–127*

gatherings, recipes for, 209–283

ginger

    Ginger–Fennel Tonic, 249

    Ginger–Turmeric Milk, 66, *67*

    Parsnip and Ginger Cake with Cultured Butter and Crème Fraîche Icing, 142–143, *143*

gluten-free bread baking tips, 105

gluten-free flour, substituting wheat flour for, 6

Gluten-Free Sourdough Starter, *58*, 59–61

Gnudi with Slow-Roasted Tomatoes, Ricotta, *246*, 247, *250*

Granola, Coconut, with Roasted Cherries, 72, *73*

Granola, Mix-and-Match, *42*, 43

Grapefruit–Carrot Juice, Spicy, 68, *69*

Greens, Bitter, on Toast with Soft-Cooked Eggs and Dukkah, *84*, 85

Greens, Rice, Sweet Potatoes, and Avocados with Crispy Chickpeas, 188, *189*

Grilled Backyard Pizzas, 253–265

Gruyère and Aioli Tartines, 240, *242*

H

Ham and Peas with Buttermilk Dressing, 160, *161*

Ham, Melon, Fennel, and Ricotta Salata, 163

hazelnuts

    Bircher Muesli with Poached Rhubarb and Hazelnuts, 74, *75*

    Chocolate–Hazelnut Butter, 29, *31*

    Dukkah, 40, *41*

    Frozen Raspberry Custard with Hazelnut Crunch, 314–315, *316–317*

    Roasted Cauliflower, Swiss Chard, and Hazelnut Pasta, 192, *193*

    Salted Hazelnut Butter Truffles, *320*, 321

Hemp Milk, 21

Herb and Flower Mayonnaise, 35

herbs, drying, 38, *39*

Hibiscus and Peach Sorbet, *310*, 311

Homemade Pasta Dinner, 227–235

Honey–Mustard Vinaigrette with Peppery Greens, 240, *243*

Hot and Spicy Mayonnaise, 35

Hummus, Red Lentil, with Roasted Carrots, 176–177, *178–179*

I

Ice Cream, No-Churn Honey, and Espresso, 312, *313*

Icing, Cultured Butter and Crème Fraîche, with Parsnip and Ginger Cake, 142–143, *143*

Icing, Sunflower Seed, with Banana Bread, 136, *137*

ingredients, 5–12

J

Juice, Spicy Carrot–Grapefruit, 68, *69*

K

kitchen tools, 12–15

L

Labneh, *36*, 37

Lamb Sausage with Yogurt, Herbs, and Fried Egg, Spicy, *202*, 203

Leek, Fennel, and Pesto Pizza, 259

Leek, Squash, and Potato Soup with Cheese Toast, *190*, 191

legumes

    Crispy Chickpeas with Rice, Sweet Potatoes, Avocados, and Greens, 188, *189*

    Lentil and Root Vegetable Stew with Broccoli Rabe and Fried Eggs, 194, *195*

    Roasted Carrots with Red Lentil Hummus, 176–177, *178–179*

    Roasted Squash Salad with White Beans, Bread Crumbs, and Preserved Lemons, 248, *251*

    Shaved Beet and Lentil Salad with Tahini and Preserved Lemon Dressing, *154*, 155

Lemons, Preserved, 48–49, *50–51*

lentils. *See* legumes

Lillet, Mashed Berries in, *265*, 265

linens, 222–223, *225*

lunch, 145–171

M

Madeleines, Orange and Brown Butter, 318, *319*

Mayonnaise, 34–35

Meatballs and Spaghetti, *196–197*, 198

Melon, Serrano, Fennel, and Ricotta Salata, 163

menus

    Celebrating with Oysters and Steak, 275

Garden and the Sea, The, 237

Grilled Backyard Pizzas, 253

Homemade Pasta Dinner, 227

Spanish Gathering, A, 213

Sunday Roasted Chicken, 267

Vegetarian Harvest Gathering, 245

milks

Coconut Milk, 21

Ginger–Turmeric Milk, 66, *67*

Hemp Milk, 21

Nut Milk, 20

Muesli with Poached Rhubarb and Hazelnuts, Bircher, 74, *75*

Mushrooms and Eggs, *166*, 167

Mustard–Honey Vinaigrette with Peppery Greens, 240, *243*

N

Nectarine, Blistered Corn, and Watercress Salad, *262*, 263

Niçoise Salad, My, *182*, 183

Nut Butter, 28

nut flour, making, 20

Nut Milk, 20

O

Olive, Caraway, and Honey Yeast Bread, Black, 110, *111*

Olive Oil and Apricot Cake, One-Bowl, 128, *129*

Olive Oil, Chocolate, and Citrus Cake, *300*, 301–302

Onion and Fennel Biscuits, Flaky Caramelized, *138*, 139–140, *141*

Onion, Tomato, and Prosciutto Pizza, Red, 258, *260–261*

Orange and Brown Butter Madeleines, 318, *319*

Oysters with Champagne Mignonette, *276*, 277–278, *278*

P

Paella, Chicken and Seafood, on an Open Fire, 214–215, *216–217*

Pancakes with Maple Yogurt, Raspberry, *94*, 95

Panna Cotta with Summer Fruits, Buttermilk, *306*, 307

pantry ingredients, 5–12

pantry staples, 17–61

Parsnip and Celery Root Mash, Crispy Snapper with, 199, *200–201*

Parsnip and Ginger Cake with Cultured Butter and Crème Fraîche Icing, 142–143, *143*

pasta

Braised Beef Ragù with Tagliatelle, *231*, 232

Homemade Pasta, 228–229, *230*

Roasted Cauliflower, Swiss Chard, and Hazelnut Pasta, 192, *193*

Spaghetti and Meatballs, *196–197*, 198

Paste, Quince, 292–293, *295*

peaches

Buttermilk Panna Cotta with Summer Fruits, *306*, 307

Grilled Peaches with Cashew Cream on Toast, *76*, 77

Peach and Hibiscus Sorbet, *310*, 311

Peach Txakoli Cocktail, 219, *221*

Sourdough Waffles with Caramelized Peaches, *90*, 91

Pears with Seed Crumble, Roasted, *286*, 303, *304–305*

Peas and Ham with Buttermilk Dressing, 160, *161*

Pepitas, Candied, 171

Pesto, Leek, and Fennel Pizza, 259

Pickled Vegetables, 44, *45*

Pie Dough 3-2-1, 114–115

Pine Nut, Fig, and Taleggio Tart, *122*, 123

Piperrada, Baked Eggs in, 86, *87*

Pistachio, Shaved Asparagus, and Cucumber Salad, *282*, 283

pizzas, *252*, *260–261*

Leek, Fennel, and Pesto Pizza, 259

Pizza Dough, 254, *255*

Squash Blossom and Ricotta Pizza, *256*, 257

Tomato, Prosciutto, and Red Onion Pizza, 258

Plum Frangipane Tart, 112, *113*

Plums, Rice Pudding with, 82, *83*

Poppy Seed–Buttermilk Vinaigrette with Radicchio, Apple, and Celery Root Salad, 233, *233*

potatoes

My Niçoise Salad, *182*, 183

Roasted Potatoes the English Way with Tarragon Aioli, 269, *270–271*

Squash, Leek, and Potato Soup with Cheese Toast, *190*, 191

Tortilla de Patatas with Romaine, Fennel, and Green Olive Salad, 184–185, *186–187*

Preserved Lemons, 48–49, *50–51*

Prosciutto, Tomato, and Red Onion Pizza, 258, *260–261*

Puff Pastry with Cultured Butter, *118*, 119–121

Q

Quince Paste, 292–293, *295*

R

Ragù with Tagliatelle, Braised Beef, *231*, 232

raspberries

Buttermilk Panna Cotta with Summer Fruits, *306*, 307

Chocolate Cream with Yogurt, Cocoa Nibs, and Raspberries, 308, *309*

Frozen Raspberry Custard with Hazelnut Crunch, 314–315, *316–317*

Mashed Berries in Lillet, 265, *265*

Raspberry Pancakes with Maple Yogurt, *94*, 95

recipe ingredients, 5–12

resources, 327–328

Rhubarb, Poached, and Hazelnuts with Bircher Muesli, 74, *75*

rice

Black Rice Bowl with Figs, Radicchio, Pickled Radishes, and Pepitas, *170*, 171

Chicken and Seafood Paella on an Open Fire, 214–215, *216–217*

Crispy Chickpeas with Rice, Sweet Potatoes, Avocados, and Greens, 188, *189*

Rice Pudding with Plums, 82, *83*

ricotta

Melon, Serrano, Fennel, and Ricotta Salata, 163

Ricotta Gnudi with Slow-Roasted Tomatoes, *246*, 247, *250*

Squash Blossom and Ricotta Pizza, *256*, 257

Romesco and Tomato Tart, 180, *181*

Root Vegetable and Lentil Stew with Broccoli Rabe and Fried Eggs, *194*, 195

Root Veggie Mash, Crispy Snapper with, 199, *200–201*

Rye–Style Seed Bread, Nordic, *100*, 101–102

S

salads

Artichoke, Fennel, Sugar Snap Pea, and Parmesan Salad, *272*, 273

Blistered Corn, Nectarine, and Watercress Salad, *262*, 263

Buttermilk-Poached Salmon Salad with Herb, Leek, and Caper Dressing, 152, *153*

Crunchy Romaine Salad with Soft Eggs and Feta, 168, *169*

Grilled Green Tomato and Eggplant Salad, 218, *220*

Melon, Serrano, Fennel, and Ricotta Salata, 163

My Niçoise Salad, *182*, 183

Peppery Greens with Mustard–Honey Vinaigrette, 240, *243*

Radicchio, Apple, and Celery Root Salad with Buttermilk–Poppy Seed Vinaigrette, 233, *233*

Roasted Squash Salad with White Beans, Bread Crumbs, and Preserved Lemons, 248, *251*

Shaved Asparagus, Cucumber, and Pistachio Salad, *282*, 283

Shaved Beet and Lentil Salad with Tahini and Preserved Lemon Dressing, *154*, 155

Spicy Chicken Salad with Apple, Celery, and Pickled Vegetables, *150*, 151

Tomato, Corn, and Bread Salad, 164, *165*

Tortilla de Patatas with Romaine, Fennel, and Green Olive Salad, 184–185, *186–187*

Winter Salad with Roasted Radicchio, Avocados, and Hazelnut Dukkah, 148, *149*

salmon. *See* fish

Salsa Verde, 199

salt, 11

sandwiches. *See* toast and open-faced sandwiches

Sausage, Spicy Lamb, with Yogurt, Herbs, and Fried Egg, *202*, 203

seafood

Chicken and Seafood Paella on an Open Fire, 214–215, *216–217*

My Mom's Fish Soup, *236*, 238–239

Oysters with Champagne Mignonette, *276*, 277–278, *278*

See also fish

Seed Butter, 28

Seed Crumble, Roasted Pears with, *286*, 303, *304–305*

seeds, collecting and drying, 38, *39*

Seedy Mayonnaise, 35

Serrano, Melon, Fennel, and Ricotta Salata, 163

settings, table, 222–223, *224–225*

Shrubs and Drinking Vinegars, *46*, 47

Smoked Salmon, Avocado, and Cucumber on Toast, *80*, 81

Snapper with Root Veggie Mash, Crispy, 199, *200–201*

Sorbet, Peach and Hibiscus, *310*, 311

soups and stews

Braised Beef Ragù with Tagliatelle, *231*, 232

Lentil and Root Vegetable Stew with Broccoli Rabe and Fried Eggs, *194*, 195

My Mom's Fish Soup, *236*, 238–239

Roasted Carrot and Cashew Soup, 158, *159*

Simple Asparagus and Avocado Soup, *156*, 157

Squash, Leek, and Potato Soup with Cheese Toast, *190*, 191

See also stocks and broths

sourdough

Gluten-Free Sourdough Starter, *58*, 59–61

Nordic Rye-Style Seed Bread, *100*, 101–102

Sourdough Boules, 103–104
Sourdough Waffles with
    Caramelized Peaches,
    90, 91
Spaghetti and Meatballs,
    196–197, 198
Spanish Gathering, A, 213–225
spices, 11–12
Spicy and Hot Mayonnaise, 35
Spicy Carrot–Grapefruit Juice,
    68, 69
Spicy Chicken Salad with Apple,
    Celery, and Pickled Vegeta-
    bles, 150, 151
Spicy Lamb Sausage with Yogurt,
    Herbs, and Fried Egg, 202, 203
squash
    Roasted Squash Brown
        Butter Cake, 134, 135
    Roasted Squash Salad with
        White Beans, Bread
        Crumbs, and Preserved
        Lemons, 248, 251
    Squash, Leek, and Potato
        Soup with Cheese Toast,
        190, 191
Squash Blossom and Ricotta
    Pizza, 256, 257
stews. See soups and stews
stocks and broths, 52
    Beef Stock, 54
    Chicken Stock, 53
    Fish Stock, 55
    Turmeric Detox Broth with
        Swiss Chard, 70, 71
    Vegetable Stock, 56, 57
strawberries
    Buttermilk Panna Cotta
        with Summer Fruits, 306,
        307
    Mashed Berries in Lillet,
        265, 265
    Strawberry Biscuits, 140
Sugar Snap Pea, Artichoke,
    Fennel, and Parmesan Salad,
    272, 273
Sunday Roasted Chicken,
    267–273
Sunflower Seed Icing, Banana
    Bread with, 136, 137

Sweet Potatoes, Rice, Avocados,
    and Greens with Crispy
    Chickpeas, 188, 189
sweeteners, 8, 11
Swiss Chard, Roasted Cauli-
    flower, and Hazelnut Pasta,
    192, 193
Swiss Chard, Turmeric Detox
    Broth with, 70, 71

T

table settings, 222–223, 224–225
Taleggio, Fig, and Pine Nut Tart,
    122, 123
Tartines, Aioli and Gruyère, 240,
    242
tarts. See baking recipes
toast and open-faced
    sandwiches
    Aioli and Gruyère Tartines,
        240, 242
    Avocado, Smoked Salmon,
        and Cucumber on Toast,
        80, 81
    Grilled Peaches with
        Cashew Cream on Toast,
        76, 77
    Mushrooms and Eggs, 166,
        167
    Soft-Cooked Eggs with
        Dukkah and Bitter Greens
        on Toast, 84, 85
    Squash, Leek, and Potato
        Soup with Cheese Toast,
        190, 191
tomatoes
    Grilled Green Tomato and
        Eggplant Salad, 218, 220
    My Niçoise Salad, 182, 183
    Ricotta Gnudi with Slow-
        Roasted Tomatoes, 246,
        247, 250
    Tomato and Romesco Tart,
        180, 181
    Tomato, Corn, and Bread
        Salad, 164, 165
    Tomato, Prosciutto, and Red
        Onion Pizza, 258, 260–261
tools, kitchen, 12–15

Tortilla de Patatas with Romaine,
    Fennel, and Green Olive Salad,
    184–185, 186–187
Tostada with Fennel, Radishes,
    and Yogurt, Egg, 88, 89
Truffles, Salted Hazelnut Butter,
    320, 321
turmeric
    Ginger–Turmeric Milk, 66, 67
    Spicy Carrot–Grapefruit
        Juice, 68, 69
    Turmeric Detox Broth with
        Swiss Chard, 70, 71

V

Vegetable Stock, 56, 57
Vegetables, Pickled, 44, 45
Vegetarian Harvest Gathering,
    245–251
Vinaigrette, Buttermilk–Poppy
    Seed, with Radicchio, Apple,
    and Celery Root Salad, 233,
    233
Vinaigrette, Mustard–Honey, with
    Peppery Greens, 240, 243
Vinegars, Drinking, 46, 47

W

Waffles with Caramelized
    Peaches, Sourdough, 90, 91
Walnuts and Dried Apricots,
    Buckwheat Sweet Yeast Bread
    with, 108, 109
Watercress, Blistered Corn, and
    Nectarine Salad, 262, 263

Y

Yogurt, Whole-Milk, 32, 33

About the Author

ARAN GOYOAGA is a cookbook author, blogger, food stylist, and photographer. Aran was born and raised in the Basque Country, in northern Spain, where her maternal grandparents owned a pastry shop and her paternal grandparents live off the land. Her blog *Cannelle et Vanille* is a two-time James Beard Award finalist. She currently lives in Seattle with her husband and two children.

Printed in China

Published by Sasquatch Books

SASQUATCH BOOKS with colophon is a registered trademark of Penguin Random House LLC

23 22 21 20 19   9 8 7 6 5 4 3 2 1

Editor: Susan Roxborough
Production editor: Bridget Sweet
Design: Anna Goldstein
Copyeditor: Rachelle Longé McGhee
Contributing writer: Jennifer McKeever Crilly
Photos: Aran Goyoaga, except for pages xii, 143, 255, 338, and back endsheet by Dorothee Brand and page 264 by Jordan Carlson

Library of Congress Cataloging-in-Publication Data
Names: Goyoaga, Aran, author.
Title: Cannelle et Vanille : nourishing, gluten-free recipes for every meal and mood / Aran Goyoaga.
Description: Seattle : Sasquatch Books, 2019.
Identifiers: LCCN 2019003267 | ISBN 9781632172006 (hardback)
Subjects: LCSH: Gluten-free diet--Recipes. | Gluten-free foods. | BISAC:
   COOKING / Health & Healing / General. | COOKING / Specific Ingre-dients /
   Natural Foods. | COOKING / Regional & Ethnic / American /
Northwestern
   States. | LCGFT: Cookbooks.
Classification: LCC RM237.86 .G68 2019 | DDC 641.5/639311--dc23
LC record available at https://lccn.loc.gov/2019003267

ISBN: 978-1-63217-200-6

Sasquatch Books
1904 Third Avenue, Suite 710 | Seattle, WA 98101
SasquatchBooks.com